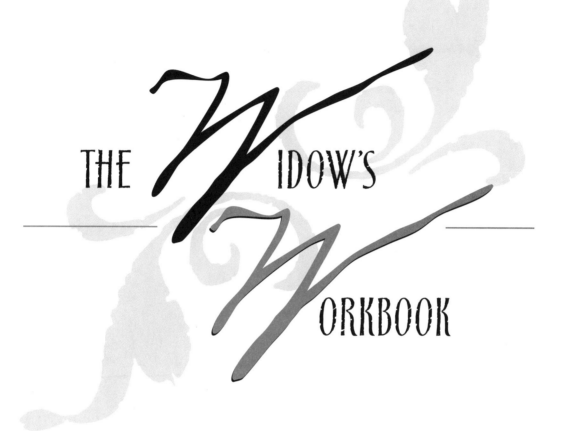

THE Widow's Workbook

A Widow's Bible Study

by

DIXIE JOHNSTON FRALEY KELLER

© 2009 Dixie Johnston Fraley Keller
This book is a revised edition of *The Widow's Workbook: A Widow's Bible Study*, first published in 2003.

Printed in the United States of America
ISBN: 978-0-89827-449-3

DEDICATION

To those left behind after September 11, 2001

. . . and the days before

. . . and the days after

. . . and Jane Denny

TABLE OF CONTENTS

ACKNOWLEDGMENTS

Nothing done alone is done in isolation. I may have written alone, but I could not have done this without the help of so many others. Glenda Morgan, my husband's assistant for years, came alongside to help me. Then I asked a fellow seminary student, Gray Keller, for help in editing. My great friends, Cheryl and Bobb Biehl, would not let a dream die. "Mr. Masterplanner" developed a plan to bring words to paper and dreams to tangible reality. He found Nathan Birky, Publisher of Premiere Publishing, and Bobbie Sease, editor extraordinaire, to breathe life into dry stacks. Graphic gurus Amy Huber (first edition) and Lyn Rayn (second edition) brought order out of chaos. You ask me how this is possible? Without God and people, it **is** impossible. To these people and so many more . . . my fellow widows, my family and friends, I give thanks—but to God I give all the glory.

PREFACE

Like so many Americans, I watched the newscasts and mourned with my country over the terrible events of September 11, 2001. My attention was focused on the firefighters, who worked heroically to find survivors in the rubble of destroyed buildings. There was such pain in my soul. Like so many others, I asked: "What could I do to help?" How could I give as much and work as hard as they were doing for life, for liberty, for love?

Since I am a widow, I decided in the midst of this horror to help other widows. I knew instinctively that many widows would emerge from this tragic day—more widows in one day from one cause than perhaps at any other time in the history of the United States. I was compelled to write a book—a workbook—to help them work through their pain. This would be my gift to them.

Thousands of miles from Ground Zero, the damaged Pentagon, and the smoking remains in a Pennsylvania field, I shuffled papers, dug into books, and began my work. In the background, the television continued its endless broadcasts, reminding me of the people I would be working for. My heart bled not only for this country, but also for the specific families who were shattered by the events of this day.

Still, I could not help but think that people lose their loved ones every day in less spectacular ways—in car accidents, in hospitals, in nursing homes. Everything that lives eventually must die. This is an undeniable certainty, the inevitability of death. We knew this when we married our husbands. We just didn't envision when or how death would make its presence known. God mercifully spared us that vision—but He did not spare us the pain once death claimed our loved one.

The first widow to make an impression on me was my Aunt Hazel. She was a strong southern lady, a true steel magnolia. My Uncle Harvey was the picture of life, big and burly, like Hoss Cartwright on *Bonanza*. He loved to have fun and lived life to the hilt. But on New Year's Day in 1974, the fun ended with a plane crash in Alabama.

This event decimated our family. I remember my father saying, as we walked in the field where the plane crashed, "It should have been me. I wished it'd been me." Even at my young age, I thought, "How do we go on? How do we recover from this?"

Twenty-five years later—another field, another plane crash, and I was the widow. This plane was a chartered Learjet with six aboard, among them golfer Payne Stewart and his agent, Robert Fraley, my husband. Departing Orlando, Florida, for Dallas, Texas, something went wrong early in the flight. Transfixed, millions watched their TV screens as the plane cruised on autopilot for nearly four hours and 1,500 miles before crashing into a field near Aberdeen, South Dakota. The official report determined that due to a gradual loss of cabin pressure, all on board died of hypoxia before the plane plummeted to earth.

Newly widowed, I asked myself the same questions I had asked following my Uncle Harvey's death: "How do I go on? How do I recover from this?"

That's where you are now. How do you go on? That's where this journey begins—asking the tough questions, looking for the real answers. Ask yourself: Where are you planning to go and where will you end up?

If life is a journey, this is now your widow's walk. It's a lonely walk, but God is with you. I wrote this book so widows would know this: **you are not alone.** Many have walked this path before you, and many will follow. Now is the time for you to start the long road of recovery. But remember, you are not alone; we are "women alone together."™

Dixie Fraley Keller
Orlando, Florida

INTRODUCTION

"He will cover you with his feathers, and under his wings
you will find refuge; his faithfulness will be your shield and rampart."
Psalm 91:4

I wrapped my arms around another widow as she wept. It may have been a normal Sunday morning in everyone else's life. But it was the first Sunday that this widow had walked into church alone.

This scene is repeated countless times on a daily basis. It is estimated that over 90 percent of women will be widowed in their lifetimes. According to the U.S. Census Bureau, 32 percent of women 55 years of age or older are widows.[1] "Nearly 700,000 women lose their husbands each year and will be widows for an average of 14 years."[2] Widows easily could qualify as a special interest group. Yet, there is no "Widows Anonymous" or "Widows United."

We don't know which is worse: to have lost the ones we loved, or to have lost the love that was given to us. Either way, we lose. We each lost the person we loved and to whom we committed our lives. We lost the love they freely gave us. Not only did we lose love, but we also lost position. Eighty percent of widows currently living in poverty were not living in poverty before their husbands died.[3] We are no longer wives. We are widows. The ones left behind. We are the ones who walk around without visible scars. Many of us do not have canes or walkers to hold us up. We are the ones who restrain our tears until we are in a private place—so that we will not "bother" anyone. We are the ones who want to yell, "This isn't fair! This isn't the way it was supposed to be!" But we remain silent. We are the ones whose hearts are gone, but whose bodies remain.

Widow. That word sounds like *window* without the "n." We feel as if people can look through us. We feel transparent. We can't hide a thing. It's not a pretty picture window. It's a dingy, fingerprinted, dirty window. We feel tainted and left out. We feel abandoned and alone. But, as I hope you will discover, we are not.

When I envisioned this book, I saw it as a Bible study for women who fall into this underserved population every year. I wanted it to be the basis for a study in a group setting, such as a church—a place where widows could come to be seen and to be heard, to learn and to lean, to absolve and be absolved, to strengthen and be strengthened. Offering this Bible study on an annual or biannual basis around the country would give ample notice to those who have been widowed or to those who know someone who might benefit from this study.

Through the timeless lens of Scripture, *A Widow's Workbook* will focus on issues relevant to widows, including:

- Loving and Losing
- Coping Skills
- Individual Grieving Processes
- Developing an Attitude of Appreciation
- Giving Back
- Living On, Loving On

You've heard the phrase, "Let your fingers do the walking," which refers to the real Yellow Pages®. Well, I hope you'll let your fingers walk through God's Word, because that is where real Truth will be found. This study, these words, are only to point you there. My discoveries, my widow's walk, are nothing in the light of walking with the real Savior for eternity. Cling to His hand and walk through His Word into His world.

Ruth 2:12 says, *"May the Lord repay you for what you have done. May you be richly rewarded by the Lord, the God of Israel, under whose wings you have come to take refuge."* These were Boaz's words to Ruth, who was a hurting and needy widow. Ruth replied, *"May I continue to find favor in your eyes, my lord . . . You have given me comfort and have spoken kindly to your servant . . ."* (v. 13).

This is my hope, to speak words of comfort kindly to His people, the widows who walk this path with me.

CHAPTER 1

LOVING

"Love bears all things, believes all things,
hopes all things, endures all things."
1 Corinthians 13:7 RSV

INTRODUCTION

You once loved and were loved. You committed your life to one human being. You thought about him constantly. Your schedule revolved around him. Now, a huge part of your life and heart has been ripped from you, without anesthesia. You chose to love . . . and now you are lost.

THINKING IT OVER

1. Why do you think human beings love?

2. Why did **you** choose to love?

3. What has the Bible taught you about love?

THINKING IN DEPTH

The following questions examine love from a scriptural perspective. Carefully read each of the Scriptures as you consider your answers to the questions. (Unless otherwise specified, Scriptures are from the NIV.)

> *"Love the Lord your God with all your heart and with all your soul and with all your strength."* Deuteronomy 6:5

1. Who are you told to love with your whole heart, soul, and strength?

> *"The commandments, 'Do not commit adultery,' 'Do not murder,' 'Do not steal,' 'Do not covet,' and whatever other commandment there may be, are summed up in this one rule: 'Love your neighbor as yourself.' Love does no harm to its neighbor. Therefore love is the fulfillment of the law.'"* Romans 13:9-10

2. How did Paul sum up the commandments?

> *"Jesus replied: 'Love the Lord your God with all your heart and with all your soul and with all your mind.' This is the first and greatest commandment. And the second is like it: 'Love your neighbor as yourself.'"* Matthew 22:37-39

3. What did Jesus say were the greatest commandments?

    a.

    b.

> *"My command is this: Love each other as I have loved you."* John 15:12

4. What did Jesus command?

"A new command I give you: Love one another. As I have loved you, so you must love one another. By this all men will know that you are my disciples, if you love one another." John 13:34-35

5. How will people know we are followers of Jesus?

"Dear friends, let us love one another, for love comes from God. Everyone who loves has been born of God and knows God. Whoever does not love does not know God, because God is love. This is how God showed his love among us: He sent his one and only Son into the world that we might live through him. This is love: not that we loved God, but that he loved us and sent his Son as an atoning sacrifice for our sins. Dear friends, since God so loved us, we also ought to love one another. No one has ever seen God; but if we love one another, God lives in us and his love is made complete in us.

"We know that we live in him and he in us, because he has given us of his Spirit. And we have seen and testify that the Father has sent his Son to be the Savior of the world. If anyone acknowledges that Jesus is the Son of God, God lives in him and he in God. And so we know and rely on the love God has for us.

"God is love. Whoever lives in love lives in God, and God in him. In this way, love is made complete among us so that we will have confidence on the day of judgment, because in this world we are like him. There is no fear in love. But perfect love drives out fear, because fear has to do with punishment. The one who fears is not made perfect in love. We love because he first loved us." 1 John 4:7-19

6. Before God told us to love Him or others, what did He do?

7. Why do we love?

" 'For I know the plans I have for you,' declares the Lord, 'plans to prosper you and not to harm you, plans to give you hope and a future.' " Jeremiah 29:11

8. God loves you. Does He have plans for you?

9. What are those plans?

    a.

    b.

    c.

    d.

"I in them and you in me. May they be brought to complete unity to let the world know that you sent me and have loved them even as you have loved me." John 17:23

10. How much does He love us?

"Father, I want those you have given me to be with me where I am, and to see my glory, the glory you have given me because you loved me before the creation of the world." John 17:24

11. How long has He loved us?

"But God demonstrates his own love for us in this: While we were still sinners, Christ died for us." Romans 5:8

12. How did God demonstrate His love for us?

"Be imitators of God, therefore, as dearly loved children and live a life of love, just as Christ loved us and gave himself up for us as a fragrant offering and sacrifice to God." Ephesians 5:1-2.

13. Because of this love, how should we live and what should we imitate? Or, better yet, how can you "live a life of love"?

14. Having studied the preceding Scriptures, do you really believe that God loves you? Why or why not?

15. Are you a better person for loving?

> "To love at all is to be vulnerable."
>
> **C. S. Lewis**

Summary

When Tennyson struggled after the death of a dear friend, he wrote: "'Tis better to have loved and lost, Than never to have loved at all."[1] Ponder this quotation as it relates to your own loss. Was it better to have loved and lost, than not to have loved at all? It is important to understand that the deeper your love, the deeper your loss and sorrow. Sometime after my husband died, I exclaimed, "Love hurts!" Nothing was truer at that moment. But I also realized nothing had blessed me so much.

Your love, your relationship, was unique. There was and will be no other "you and him." Because you loved deeply, because you cared intensely, you now feel bereft. You may be tempted to close yourself off, so that you never have to feel this searing pain again. I, too, have been tempted in this way. Lest you allow yourself to succumb to this self-imposed isolation, remember that Dostoevsky was said to have defined hell as the inability to love. Hell is a far worse situation than loss. I have always been able to shake free of this temptation by remembering love's vulnerability—not in the negative sense of defenselessness, but in the positive sense of true openness and receptivity to all love's facets. Love is a nakedness of spirit and emotion before another. Now, you just feel naked with no one there to love you. You feel naked and alone. However, the purpose of this study guide is to reaffirm that you are not alone. God is with you. Those who are studying this workbook are also with you—traveling the same path of challenge and discovery. Widowed twice, Elisabeth Elliot said, "Love always means sacrifice."[2] You have discovered this to be true for yourself. Looking at this reality in an affirming way is the particular goal set before you.

Remember, according to 1 Corinthians 13, love is the greatest thing of all things and the only eternal thing. Love transcends this world and expands in heaven. Anything done without love is wasted—both here (on earth) and there (in heaven). You have come to think of your spouse as the source of love, but we need to remember that love is of God.

My love should not depend on the object of my love, but on the source of my love. Love is the currency of eternity and an attribute of God. God is love.

> "What we have
> once enjoyed,
> we can never lose.
> All that we love
> deeply becomes
> a part of us."
>
> **Helen Keller**

"And now these three remain: faith, hope and love.
But the greatest of these is love."
1 Corinthians 13:13

CHAPTER 2

LOSING

"The Lord gave, and the Lord has taken away; blessed be the name of the Lord."
Job 1:21 RSV

INTRODUCTION

To most Americans, 9-11 has become a national day of tragedy. Widows have their own tragedy days: mine was October 25. We all have tragedy days, and we all know there may be more for us in the future. We mourn September 11 collectively, but we may mourn our own dates privately. Our losses contrast in other ways. Some losses are public, while others seem almost invisible. For example, the day you miscarried, the day you were informed you had cancer, the day you lost your job—there were no scars, you wore no bandages or cast. No one appeared to care how you were feeling.

But we care. We understand that you have loved and been loved, and that you have lost this love. So often we hear that the greater your love, the greater your loss. Maybe that explains why the word passion means to suffer.[1]

THINKING IT OVER

1. Describe how you handle your tragedy days.

2. After the 9-11 attack, I heard a woman from New York say, "I just keep waiting for him to walk through the door and make everything okay." I had these same thoughts after my tragedy day. What are your thoughts?

3. What are you doing with your thoughts and longings? Do you share them with anyone? Do you journal?

THINKING IN DEPTH

In *A Grace Disguised*, Jerry Sittser describes the loss of his mother, wife, and four-year-old daughter in an automobile accident.[2] This man knows about loss. He reminds us that loss is a **universal** experience, although each experience is **unique**. He concludes, it is "the experience of loss that becomes the defining moment of our lives, for that is as inevitable as death, which is that last loss awaiting us all. It is how we respond to loss that matters."[3]

Through Sittser's eyes, we learn the following about loss:[4]

- Loss can make us more_____.
  (You fill in the blank.)
- Loss requires we live in a delicate tension (mourn/live)
- Loss provides an opportunity to:
  - take inventory
  - consider priorities
  - determine a new direction
- Loss establishes a new context for life
- Loss became part of our story
- Loss strips us of the props we rely on
- Loss has revealed how small my life is and how limited my resources are
- Loss turns life into a snapshot
- Loss puts a sudden halt to business as usual
- Loss takes what we might do and turns it into what we can never do
- Loss forces us to see ourselves for what we are
- Loss can be transformative if we set a new course
- Loss has little to do with our notion of fairness
- Loss deprives us of control
- Loss may call the existence of God into question
- Loss reminds us that we do not have the final word
- Loss leads to pain that forces us to acknowledge our mortal fate
- Loss is a universal experience
- Loss is also a solitary experience
- Loss reduces people to a state of almost total brokenness and vulnerability
- Loss is not a once-in-a-lifetime experience
- Loss can diminish us, but it can also expand us
- Loss can function as a catalyst to transform us

1. Picking up on the universality and uniqueness of loss, are **you** any different in experiencing loss?

2. How is this loss unique for you?

3. Have you lost something no one else has ever lost?

4. According to Gerald Sittser, who experiences loss?

5. 1 Peter 4:7 says, *"The end of all things is near. Therefore be clear minded and self-controlled so that you can pray."* Therefore, we should be:

    a.

    b.

    c. so that we can _____.

6. If loss is a part of life, how can we understand this and—if not appreciate it—learn from it?

7. How has this loss affected your life?

"The great thing, if one can, is to stop regarding all the unpleasant things as interruptions of one's 'own' or 'real' life. The truth is of course that what one calls the interruptions are precisely one's real life—the life God is sending one day by day: what one calls one's 'real life' is a phantom of one's own imagination."

C. S. Lewis

8. How would you like it to change your life?

9. How would you like this loss to affect your family?

10. What have you learned about yourself because of this loss?

11. Read the C. S. Lewis quote in the sidebar. Does your loss feel real or unreal?

12. What are you learning from this pain and separation?

13. Tim Hansel said, "If your security is based on something that can be taken away from you—you will constantly be on a false edge of security."[5] How do you identify with this statement?

14. What people or experiences are you encountering during your time of loss? What is your part in making these encounters positive or negative?

SUMMARY

How two become one is a mystery. But when the one becomes a half, it's almost unbearable. You do feel as if you've been torn in half. Still, even as you experience the pain of this loss, you instinctively want to be a whole person. You feel incomplete somehow, and so utterly alone.

Read the following Scriptures, paying particular attention to the underlined phrases (my emphasis):

> *"Say among the nations, 'The Lord reigns.' The world is firmly established, it cannot be moved; <u>he will judge the peoples with equity</u>."* Psalm 96:10

> *"This will take place <u>on the day when God will judge men's secrets</u> through Jesus Christ, as my gospel declares."* Romans 2:16

> *"In the presence of God and of Christ Jesus, <u>who will judge the living and the dead</u>, and in view of his appearing and his kingdom, I give you this charge . . ."* 2 Timothy 4:1

> *"And I saw the dead, great and small, standing before the throne, and books were opened. Another book was opened, which is the book of life. <u>The dead were judged according to what they had done as recorded in the books</u>."* Revelation 20:12

Did it ever occur to you that you will not go before God's judgment throne as half of a couple or as part of a family? You will go before the King alone, as an individual. The aloneness you are now feeling as a widow is the aloneness you will experience before the throne of God. Just as you came into the world alone, you will enter the throne room alone. You alone are accountable to God for your actions in this life, not theirs.

Has the loss that overshadows every minute of your day given you a new perspective on what it means to be alone? Losing infers you had something. We lose sight of the fact that people and things are not ours, and they are certainly not immortal. Being alone is not the end of life; it is the start of a new life. Being alone does not dictate being lonely. God will meet you there (Joshua 1:9). In *The Purpose Driven Life*, Rick Warren says, "Real security can only be found in that which can never be taken from you—your relationship with God."[6]

> *"I consider everything a loss compared to the surpassing greatness of knowing Christ Jesus my Lord . . ."*
> Philippians 3:8

"Security is found by fixing our hope on God, who gives us everything we need."

Don and Sally Meredith

NOTES

CHAPTER 3

LIVING

"I tell you the truth, whoever hears my word and believes him who sent me has eternal life and will not be condemned; he has crossed over from death to life."
John 5:24

INTRODUCTION

How many times have you heard the expression, "Life is a gift"? Does that statement sound different now that the gift (your husband) has been recalled? We don't easily relinquish gifts, do we? In that respect, we haven't changed much since we were children.

THINKING IT OVER

1. Has your experience with death caused you to question God and His love for you?

2. Do you sometimes doubt your purpose in life, now that the "props" have been knocked out from under you? Are you sometimes resentful that your life has taken this turn, which seems so far off the path you thought was laid out before you?

THINKING IN DEPTH

The following questions examine three aspects of life from a scriptural perspective: 1) earthly life versus eternal life; 2) the quality of life; and 3) the uniqueness of life. Carefully read each of the Scriptures as you consider your answers to the questions.

I. THE PERSPECTIVE OF LIFE: EARTHLY V. ETERNAL

> *"For we are God's workmanship, created in Christ Jesus to do good works, which God prepared in advance for us to do."* Ephesians 2:10

1. According to Ephesians 2:10:

   a. Who made us?

   b. Why were we created?

   c. When were these plans made?

> *"And he is not served by human hands, as if he needed anything, because he himself gives all men life and breath and everything else."* Acts 17:25

2. According to Acts 17:25, who gives life?

> *"The thief comes only to steal and kill and destroy; I have come that they may have life, and have it to the full."* John 10:10

3. According to John 10:10, who gives a **full** life?

> *"Show me, O Lord, my life's end and the number of my days; let me know how fleeting is my life."* Psalm 39:4

4. Since our lives have an end, what should we do, according to Psalm 39:4?

   a.

   b.

5. What do you think the psalmist means by calling life "fleeting"?

"Each man's life is but a breath." Psalm 39:5b

"Why, you do not even know what will happen tomorrow. What is your life? You are a mist that appears for a little while and then vanishes." James 4:14

6. In Psalm 39:5 and James 4:14, what metaphors are used to describe life?

a.

b.

"Now this is eternal life: that they may know you, the only true God, and Jesus Christ, whom you have sent." John 17:3

"And this is the testimony: God has given us eternal life, and this life is in his Son." 1 John 5:11

"We know also that the Son of God has come and has given us understanding, so that we may know him who is true. And we are in him who is true—even in his Son Jesus Christ. He is the true God and eternal life." 1 John 5:20

7. According to John 17:3 and 1 John 5:11, 20, **what** is eternal life and **when** does it start?

". . . that everyone who believes in him may have eternal life." John 3:15

"For God so loved the world that he gave his one and only Son, that whoever believes in him shall not perish but have eternal life." John 3:16

"Do not work for food that spoils, but for food that endures to eternal life, which the Son of Man will give you." John 6:27a

"For my Father's will is that everyone who looks to the Son and believes in him shall have eternal life, and I will raise him up at the last day." John 6:40

*"I tell you the truth, he who believes **has** everlasting life."* John 6:47 [my emphasis]

"I am the living bread that came down from heaven. If anyone eats of this bread, he will live forever. This bread is my flesh, which I will give for the life of the world." John 6:51

8. According to the preceding Scriptures, **who** has eternal life?

". . . so that, having been justified by his grace, we might become heirs having the hope of eternal life." Titus 3:7

9. How are we justified to have eternal life?

"Truly, truly, I say to you, he who hears My word, and believes Him who sent Me, has eternal life, and does not come into judgment, but has passed out of death into life." John 5:24 NASB

"I give them eternal life, and they shall never perish; no one can snatch them out of my hand." John 10:28

10. What will happen to those who have eternal life?

"For we who are alive are always being given over to death for Jesus' sake, so that his life may be revealed in our mortal body. So then, death is at work in us, but life is at work in you." 2 Corinthians 4:11-12

11. According to 2 Corinthians 4:11-12:

   a. What can our life reveal?

   b. What is at work in us?

"Multitudes who sleep in the dust of the earth will awake: some to everlasting life, others to shame and everlasting contempt." Daniel 12:2

"Then they will go away to eternal punishment, but the righteous to eternal life." Matthew 25:46

12. According to Daniel 12:2 and Matthew 25:46, is there a difference between the death of believers and unbelievers?

"Keep yourselves in God's love as you wait for the mercy of our Lord Jesus Christ to bring you to eternal life." Jude 21

13. What should we do as we wait for this gift of eternal life?

14. How can you live in that way?

"Clearly no one is justified before God by the law, because, 'The righteous will live by faith.'" Galatians 3:11

"Since we live by the Spirit, let us keep in step with the Spirit." Galatians 5:25

15. The verses from Galatians above give us two things to live by:

a. Galatians 3:11 _____ (See also Romans 1:17 and
   2 Corinthians 5:7.)

b. Galatians 5:25 _____

"For to be sure, he was crucified in weakness, yet he lives by God's power. Likewise, we are weak in him, yet by God's power we will live with him to serve you." 2 Corinthians 13:4

16. What else enables us to live, according to 2 Corinthians 13:4?

> "Everyone dies. Not everyone really lives."
>
> **Unknown**

II. THE QUALITY OF LIFE

Jonathan Swift said, "May you live all the days of your life." A quote from the Roman philosopher Seneca expands on this thought: "As long as you live, keep learning how to live." How easy it is to quote these maxims to others who may be experiencing loss. But how difficult it is to hear someone quote these "platitudes" to *you* in your time of loss. The idea of carrying on "life as usual" may seem callous and unrealistic to you. The pain is too sharp, the memory of death too intense. But to continue to live life to the fullest—not partially, not half-heartedly—will be your greatest challenge. I think the greatest tragedy is not death, but a life not lived.

Perhaps you have decided that the only way you can "get through life" is to put aside all thoughts of death. But, forgetting death tempts us to lose perspective.

> *"[2] As God lives, who has taken away my right, and the Almighty, who has made my soul bitter; [3] as long as my breath is in me, and the spirit of God is in my nostrils; [4] my lips will not speak falsehood, and my tongue will not utter deceit . . . [5] till I die I will not put away my integrity from me. [6] I hold fast my righteousness, and will not let it go; my heart does not reproach me for any of my days."*
> Job 27:2-6 RSV

17. Job 27:2-6 RSV can teach us some things about how to live.

    a. According to verse 3, how long are we to maintain righteousness?

    b. According to verse 4, what are we not to do?

    c. According to verse 5, what are we to uphold until death?

    d. According to verse 6, what are we to maintain and never let go of?

18. Considering verse 6, do you "reproach" any of your days? Do you blame others or yourself for what happened? Do you resent or regret being left behind?

> "Life can only be understood backwards, but it must be lived forward."
>
> **Søren Kierkegaard**

19. How can you check these feelings of reproach?

> ***Nevertheless I live****; yet not I, but Christ liveth in me: and the life which I now live in the flesh I live by the faith of the Son of God, who loved me, and gave himself for me."* Galatians 2:20 KJV [my emphasis]

> *". . . known, yet regarded as unknown; dying, and yet we live on; beaten, and yet not killed . . ."* 2 Corinthians 6:9

During my worst days, when I could barely get out of bed, I would repeat the words of Galatians 2:20. Reciting this Scripture every morning enabled me to get up from my bed and get out into the world. The phrase, "nevertheless I live," is picked up again in 2 Corinthians 6:9 ("yet we live on").

20. Do you feel as if you are both dying and living [the paradox of looking alive on the outside, but feeling dead on the inside]?

"The thief comes only to steal and kill and destroy; I have come that they may have life, and have it to the full." John 10:10

"In the same way, count yourselves dead to sin but alive to God in Christ Jesus." Romans 6:11

Anything that tries to focus our attention on death instead of life, on what we do not have, rather than what we do have, is a thief—robbing us of life.

21. According to Romans 6:11, what are we alive to?

"Do not offer the parts of your body to sin, as instruments of wickedness, but rather offer yourselves to God, as those who have been brought from death to life; and offer the parts of your body to him as instruments of righteousness." Romans 6:13

22. Then, according to Romans 6:13, what should we do?

23. How can you be an instrument of righteousness?

"When you were dead in your sins and in the uncircumcision of your sinful nature, God made you alive with Christ. He forgave us all our sins . . ." Colossians 2:13

"For whoever finds me finds life and receives favor from the Lord." Proverbs 8:35

24. From reading Colossians 2:13 and Proverbs 8:35, who makes us alive?

"He who has the Son has life; he who does not have the Son of God does not have life. I write these things to you who believe in the name of the Son of God so that you may know that you have eternal life." 1 John 5:12-13

25. How do we know if we have life, according to 1 John 5:12-13?

"And he died for all, that those who live should no longer live for themselves but for him who died for them and was raised again." 2 Corinthians 5:15

26. According to 2 Corinthians 5:15, should we live for ourselves?

"He himself bore our sins in his body on the tree, so that we might die to sins and live for righteousness;* by his wounds you have been healed." 1 Peter 2:24

[*righteousness—we'll define as **rightly relating** (to God, others, and things)]

27. What should we live for?

"[35] So do not throw away your confidence; it will be richly rewarded. [36] You need to persevere so that when you have done the will of God, you will receive what he has promised. [37] For in just a very little while, 'He who is coming will come and will not delay. [38] But my righteous one will live by faith. And if he shrinks back, I will not be pleased with him.' " Hebrews 10:35-38

28. What would please God in our living? See Hebrews 10:35-38.

a.

b.

c.

d.

"It ought to be the business of every day to prepare for our last day."

Matthew Henry

"Therefore, I urge you, brothers, in view of God's mercy, to offer your bodies as living sacrifices, holy and pleasing to God—this is your spiritual act of worship." Romans 12:1

29. How does Paul urge us to live in Romans 12:1?

"And if the Spirit of him who raised Jesus from the dead is living in you, he who raised Christ from the dead will also give life to your mortal bodies through his Spirit, who lives in you." Romans 8:11

30. If God lives within you, what will happen, according to Romans 8:11?

31. You are looking at your life as it is now, but can you look back and see God's goodness and hand at different junctures in your life? Give examples.

III. THE UNIQUENESS OF LIFE

So often we overlook the uniqueness of all of God's creation. Not only is your fingerprint unique, but so is your face, your personality, your history, and even your invisible DNA. Even a snowflake, which is literally here for a breath and then gone—something so finite, so limited, so fragile—is utterly unique. Why would God go to such trouble to create billions and billions of snowflakes, most of which we'll never see, and yet not create two snowflakes alike? That is because God is in the business of uniqueness. Intricate detail is part of His character. He loves uniqueness. He treasures individuality. He custom-makes everything in creation—with distinction.

"I wish that all men were as I am. But each man has his own gift from God; one has this gift, another has that." 1 Corinthians 7:7

"Each one should use whatever gift he has received to serve others, faithfully administering God's grace in its various forms." 1 Peter 4:10

"If anyone speaks, he should do it as one speaking the very words of God. If anyone serves, he should do it with the strength God provides, so that in all things God may be praised through Jesus Christ." 1 Peter 4:11

32. First Corinthians 7:7 tells us that each person has his/her own gift from God.

a. According to 1 Peter 4:10 what should we do with that gift?

"We must care for our bodies as though we were going to live forever. But we must care for our souls as if we were going to die tomorrow."

Attributed to St. Augustine

b. According to 1 Peter 4:11, how are you enabled to use your gift?

c. Why are you to use your gift? What is its purpose?

"[7] But to each one of us grace has been given as Christ apportioned it. [8] This is why it says: 'When he ascended on high, he led captives in his train and gave gifts to men'. . . [11] It was he who gave some to be apostles, some to be prophets, some to be evangelists, and some to be pastors and teachers, [12] to prepare God's people for works of service, so that the body of Christ may be built up [13] until we all reach unity in the faith and in the knowledge of the Son of God and become mature, attaining to the whole measure of the fullness of Christ." Ephesians 4:7-8, 11-13

33. Ephesians 4:7-13 sheds more light on this subject.

a. What does verse 7 tell us that we have been given?

b. How has it been given?

c. Why has it been given (verse 12)?

d. What does verse 13 tell us we will become?

SUMMARY

We began this chapter by looking at the phrase, "Life is a gift." It is human nature—evident in the smallest of children—to balk at relinquishing gifts. When the gift of a spouse was taken from us, we experienced the full gamut of emotions, from anger to resentment to reproach to doubt. Through the experience of this loved one's death, by sharing our experiences with one another **through the filter of God's Word**, we are learning to view life with a different perspective. We are coming to a greater understanding of the contrast between earthly life and eternal life. We are beginning to enhance our quality of life, seeing each new day as a gift, as something filled with endless possibilities. And we are learning that we are each unique, a handcrafted creation precious to God. God gave us the gift of life and eternal life through His Son. Our challenge is to live our lives, as we unwrap our gifts daily, *"so that in all things God may be praised through Jesus Christ"* (1 Peter 4:11).

"We were therefore buried with him through baptism into death in order that, just as Christ was raised from the dead through the glory of the Father, we too may live a new life."
Romans 6:4

CHAPTER 4

DYING

"For to me, to live is Christ and to die is gain."
Philippians 1:21

INTRODUCTION

"Death is the debt we all must pay." Those words of Euripides are just as relevant today as they were in ancient Greece. Death is inevitable. And, as I realized through the death of my husband, death is so final. It's the most final thing I have ever experienced. Death not only is final, it also is universal. No one escapes it.

But there are parameters to its finality. We've often heard it said, "Death is not a period, but a comma." Gigi Blalock, a special friend who is also a widow, phrases her comment more eloquently, "Death is the last chapter in time, but the first chapter in eternity." My professor, Bruce Waltke, puts it this way, "Death is god in the unbeliever. Life is the last word to the believer."

At one funeral I attended, the priest said, "Death doesn't have the last word." I knew on an intellectual level what the priest meant, but in the depths of my emotions, it sure felt as if death were having the last word. The priest said it again, "Death does not have the last word. *Love does.*" Those last two words make all the difference.

THINKING IT OVER

1. Does death have a purpose?

2. Can anything good come from death?

3. How can death be a testimony to God's glory?

THINKING IN DEPTH

The following questions examine two aspects of death from a scriptural perspective: 1) death's certainty, and 2) death's witness. Carefully read each of the Scriptures as you consider your answers to the questions.

DEATH'S CERTAINTY: "DUST TO DUST"

Genesis 3:19 tells us that death is a curse, the direct result of sin. God tells Adam that he came from dust and that he will return to dust—along with all his descendants. Job echoes this: *"Naked I came . . . and naked I will depart. The Lord gave and the Lord has taken away; may the name of the Lord be praised"* (Job 1:21).

Have you ever thought of that phrase, "dust to dust," when you are dusting and cleaning your house? It hit me one day. Something that I fight every day—something I am even allergic to—is what the Bible says we came from and will go back to.

- *"Then the Lord God formed man of dust. . ."* Genesis 2:7 RSV

- *"For He Himself knows our frame; He is mindful that we are but dust."* Psalm 103:14 NASB

- *"All go to the same place; all come from dust, and to dust all return."* Ecclesiastes 3:20

Dusting is an endless chore. It seems that as soon as you finish dusting, the dust has already begun to settle on the furniture again. Like dust, death is ever with us. It is constant. The only difference now with death is that it is at your house. It is your loved one. It is your loss. Like dust, the death of your loved one seems to hang in the air, swirl around you, and settle on everything you touch. It infiltrates every crevice in your house, penetrates every pore of your skin. You breathe it in and exhale it. Death seems to cover everything. Living with death is like living with dust. The question is, how do you go on, in spite of it? How do you fight it, deal with it, and live on, in spite of it?

"It is better to go to a house of mourning than to go to a house of feasting, for death is the destiny of every man; the living should take this to heart." Ecclesiastes 7:2

1. In Ecclesiastes 7:2, who escapes death?

"No man has power over the wind to contain it; so no one has power over the day of his death." Ecclesiastes 8:8a

2. In Ecclesiastes 8:8a, do we have any power over the day of our death?

> "Time presupposes change and change is a kind of death."
>
> **St. Augustine**

"For the living know that they will die, but the dead know nothing . . ."
Ecclesiastes 9:5a

3. In Ecclesiastes 9:5a, what should the living know with certainty?

"But now that he is dead, why should I fast? Can I bring him back again? I will go to him, but he will not return to me." 2 Samuel 12:23

4. According to 2 Samuel 12:23, can you do anything about the death of a loved one?

"For the wages of sin is death, but the gift of God is eternal life in Christ Jesus our Lord." Romans 6:23

5. In Romans 6:23:

   a. What is the cost of sin?

   b. What is the gift of God?

"Precious in the sight of the Lord is the death of his saints." Psalm 116:15

6. According to Psalm 116:15, does God care about the death of His loved ones?

"For I am convinced that neither death nor life, neither angels nor demons, neither the present nor the future, nor any powers, neither height nor depth, nor anything else in all creation, will be able to separate us from the love of God that is in Christ Jesus our Lord." Romans 8:38-39

7. According to Romans 8:38-39, can death separate us from God's love?

"The righteous perish, and no one ponders it in his heart; devout men are taken away, and no one understands that the righteous are taken away to be spared from evil."
Isaiah 57:1

8. Isaiah 57:1 tells us:

  a. We may not always _____ why our loved ones die.

  b. We learn that they are taken away to be spared from _____.

"Then they will go away to eternal punishment, but the righteous to eternal life."
Matthew 25:46

9. After death, according to Matthew 25:46, what happens to those who are righteous?

"I tell you the truth, whoever hears my word and believes him who sent me has eternal life and will not be condemned; he has crossed over from death to life."
John 5:24

10. What three things does John 5:24 tell us about those who believe in Christ?

"He is not the God of the dead, but of the living, for to him all are alive." Luke 20:38

11. According to Luke 20:38:

  a. Is God the God of the living or of the dead?

  b. Who is alive to God?

"[7] For none of us lives to himself alone and none of us dies to himself alone. [8] If we live, we live to the Lord; and if we die, we die to the Lord. So, whether we live or die, we belong to the Lord." Romans 14:7-8

12. According to Romans 14:7-8:

  a. Who lives or dies alone?

  b. Who do we belong to, whether we live or die?

"[54] When the perishable has been clothed with the imperishable, and the mortal with immortality, then the saying that is written will come true: 'Death has been swallowed up in victory.' [55] 'Where, O death, is your victory? Where, O death, is your sting?' [56] The sting of death is sin, and the power of sin is the law. [57] But thanks be to God! He gives us the victory through our Lord Jesus Christ. [58] Therefore, my dear brothers, stand firm. Let nothing move you. Always give yourselves fully to the work of the Lord, because you know that your labor in the Lord is not in vain."
1 Corinthians 15:54-58

13. According to 1 Corinthians 15:57, who gives us victory over death?

14. Therefore, according to verse 58, what should we do?

    a. _____ _____

    b. Let _____ move you.

    c. _____ give yourself _____ to the **work** of the Lord, because you know that your **labor** (notice how the word *labor* matches the word *work* in the previous phrase) in the Lord is not in vain.

    "Just as man is destined to die once, and after that to face judgment . . ."
    Hebrews 9:27

15. In Hebrews 9:27, how many times does one have to die?

    "There is an appointed time for everything. And there is a time for every event under heaven—a time to give birth, and a time to die; a time to plant, and a time to uproot what is planted." Ecclesiastes 3:1-2 NASB

16. After reading the verses from Ecclesiastes:

    a. What do you learn about the timing of every event under heaven?

    b. Then, does death have a purpose?

    c. Have you ever thought of death as an appointment? What is your reaction to the quotation from Ravi Zacharias, that death "is a moment that the Bible says has been set for each of us"?

"Death is the moment we all seek to flee, yet it is a moment that the Bible says has been set for each of us before it ever comes to be."

Ravi Zacharias

"And even the very hairs of your head are all numbered." Matthew 10:30

17. According to Matthew 10:30, God has not only numbered your days, what else has He counted?

"[20] I eagerly expect and hope that I will in no way be ashamed, but will have sufficient courage so that now as always Christ will be exalted in my body, whether by life or by death. [21] For to me, to live is Christ and to die is gain."
Philippians 1:20-21

18. What did Paul say about the prospect of dying in Philippians 1:21?

DEATH'S WITNESS

Can anything good come from death? Jesus said in John 12:24: *"I tell you the truth, unless a kernel of wheat falls to the ground and dies, it remains only a single seed. But if it dies, it produces many seeds."*

This Scripture speaks vividly to me. You see, when my husband and his friends crashed into a field in South Dakota, they were traveling faster than the speed of sound. Their bodies were scattered across the field. I saw this as a picture of seeds being scattered on the earth. I saw their lives being "sown" and we were the ones reaping a harvest from what they left behind. From the death of my husband and his friends, I saw the possibility of life for others. That is how I saw good coming from the death of my loved one. You may need to look at things differently to see how good can come from your loss.

"Truly, truly, I say to you, unless a grain of wheat falls into the earth and dies, it remains by itself alone; but if it dies, it bears much fruit." John 12:24 NASB

19. After reading John 12:24 again, this time in the NASB, what do you learn about death?

A lot of wise people have had a lot to say on the subject of death. The following quotes offer insights that may help to alter your perspective on death.

- "His miracle is not to be there to keep us from dying. It is to take us through death into His eternal presence, which is the place of ultimate communion." Ravi Zacharias[1]

- "It is only the denial of death that allows us to continue rebelling against God."[2] Blaise Pascal

- ". . . use death to teach themselves how to live."[3] Pascal

- "Remember death acts like a filter, helping us to hold on to the essential and let go of the trivial."[4] Pascal

- "Death not only filters our priorities, it also filters our passions."[5] Pascal

- "Labor now to live so, that at the hour of death thou mayest rather rejoice than fear."[6] Thomas à Kempis

- "Death begins a wicked man's hell, but it puts an end to a godly man's hell."[7] Thomas Watson

- "Death is a triumphant chariot, to carry every child of God to his Father's mansion."[8] Thomas Watson

- "Through conversion, we enter into the kingdom of God; through death we enter into the glory of God." Richard Baxter

- "May the Lord teach us what it means to live in terms of the end."[9] Jim Elliot

- "What is death? It is not a condition but a transition; not an abiding place, but a passage; not a house, but a doorway." F. B. Meyer

- "Those without Christ face a hopeless end; those with Christ look forward to an endless hope."[10] The Closer Walk New Testament

20. Did any of these quotations speak to you personally? If so, in what way?

"For when David had served God's purpose in his own generation, he fell asleep; he was buried with his fathers and his body decayed." Acts 13:36

21. According to Acts 13:36, when David "had served God's purpose in his own generation," what happened to him?

22. What does this tell you about God's plan for **your** spouse?

"Death contributes something decisive to the meaning of life."

Thomas Merton

23. What does this tell you about God's plan for **you**?

"By faith Abel offered God a better sacrifice than Cain did. By faith he was commended as a righteous man, when God spoke well of his offerings. And by faith he still speaks, even though he is dead." Hebrews 11:4

24. Hebrews 11:4 doesn't mean that the dead literally can "still speak." What does this verse mean?

SUMMARY

To me, Hebrews 11:4 is just plain exciting! I discovered that the dead can still have a witness by the faith they lived out while with us. This passage tells us that the lives of our loved ones are still a witness in our minds and hearts. This is especially true in how we decide to live as a result of the influence of their lives. My spouse's life of faith still lives on in how I now conduct my life in memory of him.

Hebrews 11:4 also teaches a lesson about love's durability. In my marriage vows, I pledged "'til death do us part." First Corinthians 13:8 tells us, *"love never fails."* In verse 13 we read that faith, hope, and love remain (abide KJV), but *"the greatest of these is love."* Even though death has torn us apart, taken my loved one from me, I understand with new insight how love can go on forever. Our loved ones are gone, but the love we feel for them has not departed.

Proverbs 10:7a says, *"The memory of the righteous will be a blessing."* It is my hope that your memory of your spouse is a blessing indeed! While you may not yet notice any blessings from the death of your spouse, begin to pray that the Lord will allow your spouse's death to be a testimony of God's glory.

"Precious in the sight of the
Lord is the death of his saints."
Psalm 116:15

DEATH

Death comes to us all
Death makes us fall
On our knees to You, O Lord
We're on our knees before You, O Lord

For we don't know what to do
But our eyes are upon You
Cause this death has struck us in the heart
We don't know where to go or how to start

Death comes to us all
Death makes us crawl
On our knees to You, O Jesus
Please come and comfort us

Cause death comes knocking on our door
It keeps knocking wanting more and more
And we are tired, confused, and angry
O God, come quick to help me

For where is the hope in the midst of despair
Where are those who really are supposed to care
I am dying in my heart and soul
Cause this death has left me in a hole

But though it may seem more than you can bear
Please know that Jesus our Lord is there
To give you hope and to give you life
In the midst of grief's horrific strife.

Steven Gray Keller ©
Used by Permission

NOTES

CHAPTER 5

FEELING

"Cast all your anxiety on him because he cares for you."
1 Peter 5:7

INTRODUCTION

Death introduces you to feelings you may never have experienced before. Through the grieving process, you will begin to feel like a clearinghouse of emotions . . . you will feel avalanched by emotions. Seemingly contradictory emotions will collide internally, causing you to feel that your life is some kind of bizarre dichotomy—a crazy quilt of torn pieces that do not fit together. Pummeled by so many different emotions at so many different concentrations of intensity, you may feel overwhelmed to the point of ambivalence—not knowing what you are supposed to be "feeling" at any given moment.

THINKING IT OVER

1. Why do you think God allows pain?

2. Is it wrong to question God about the circumstances in your life?

3. What is your dominant feeling now?

THINKING IN DEPTH

Before we embark on a personal study of feelings as they relate to the death of a loved one, read what some others have said about the part emotions play in our lives:

- "Emotions are one of the least reliable yet most influential forces in our lives."[1] Steven Estes and Joni Eareckson Tada

- "Emotion without truth produces empty frenzy and cultivates shallow people."[2] John Piper

- "Everything we feel should be the result of the way we think."[3] Don Kistler

- "We learn to live not by our feelings about God but by the facts of God."[4] Eugene Peterson

In this chapter we will look at some of the emotions you may be experiencing at this time. We cannot possibly cover every feeling involved in the loss of a loved one, but will focus on twelve primary emotions. As we examine these from a scriptural perspective, see which Scriptures speak to you specifically.

Pain

After the terrible desecration of September 11, 2001, Ravi Zacharias commented, "We have not seen the end of pain. It is part of the cost of caring and loving."[5] Years ago C. S. Lewis said, "God whispers to us in our pleasures, speaks in our conscience, but shouts in our pain: it is His megaphone to rouse a deaf world."[6]

Right now, I know the megaphone is hurting not only your ears, but your very being. This shouting reaches to your inner depths. You want it to quit.

Someone has said that our lives are the same in that they are temporary—only the quality and the length of our time make our lives different. The choice for all of us is not if we will accept pain, but how we will accept it. Tim Hansel talks about the circle of pain in our lives: "Pain is inevitable, but misery is optional. We cannot avoid pain, but we can avoid joy . . . Pain is a part of the process . . . from the shedding of blood that initiates birth to the last gasp of astonishment in the face of death, we are encircled in suffering."[7]

Pain, internally or externally, emotionally or physically, is about us and how we feel—about how this pain makes us feel. Philip Yancey said, "Pain narrows vision. The most private of sensations, it forces us to think of ourselves and little else."[8] This brings it home. We don't want to feel pain. Not even a little bit. It overshadows everything and hurts too much. It reminds us too much of death. However, just as we saw in the previous chapter that death has a purpose, we will see that pain and the other emotions we are experiencing now have a purpose. Jerry Bridges tells us, "God never allows pain without a purpose."[9] Ney Bailey asked rhetorically, "Is my God bigger than my hurt?"[10]

"The only way to transform pain is to experience it."

Paula D'Arcy

Pain first appears in Genesis 3:16 as the consequence of man's disobedience to God. Job also was very well acquainted with pain. Like Job, the prophet Jeremiah even questioned God about it, *"Why is my pain unending?"* (Jeremiah 15:18).

"For it is commendable if a man bears up under the pain of unjust suffering because he is conscious of God." 1 Peter 2:19

1. What does 1 Peter 2:19 say about pain?

"He will wipe every tear from their eyes. There will be no more death or mourning or crying or pain, for the old order of things has passed away." Revelation 21:4

2. What does Revelation 21:4 say about pain?

Bitterness/Resentment

In that avalanche of emotions I mentioned at the beginning of the chapter, you may be feeling bitterness or resentment on top of pain. Sometimes, the resentment comes as the result of pain. Bitterness is a robber. It robs you of peace. It robs you of joy. It robs you of fellowship. Worse still, it is contagious. Someone has said that bitterness "is simply the result of not seeing suffering from God's perspective."

"See to it that no one misses the grace of God and that no bitter root grows up to cause trouble and defile many." Hebrews 12:15

3. According to Hebrews 12:15:

a. What does bitterness do?

b. What can bitterness make us miss?

"Get rid of all bitterness, rage and anger, brawling and slander, along with every form of malice. Be kind and compassionate to one another, forgiving each other, just as in Christ God forgave you." Ephesians 4:31-32

4. According to Ephesians 4:31-32:

a. What are we to do with bitterness?

"Bitterness is a lack of forgiveness multiplied many times over, taking root and spreading into every segment of life . . . Bitterness is a wrong response and is never acceptable to God."

Charles Stanley

b. Then what are we urged to do?

5. Do you agree or disagree with Elisabeth Elliot's suggestion that depression may be the result of bitterness? Why?

Bitterness does not stop at robbing you of peace and joy. It invades other areas of your life. Bitterness is like a greenhouse in which conditions are perfect for growing many destructive attitudes and emotions.

Disappointment

Like other negative emotions, disappointment feeds on itself, creating a cycle of frustration and failure. It causes you to be so inwardly focused that you sometimes fail to see the way out.

> *"And hope does not disappoint us, because God has poured out his love into our hearts by the Holy Spirit, whom he has given us."* Romans 5:5

> *"They cried to you and were saved; in you they trusted and were not disappointed."* Psalm 22:5

6. According to the two Scriptures above, what does not disappoint?

a. Romans 5:5

b. Psalm 22:5

7. Skip Heitzig said, "Disappointments can sometimes be God's appointments." What do you think he meant by that?

Discouragement

We know that even Jesus became discouraged. Twice at Gethsemane He asked His Father to take the cup (of suffering) away (Matthew 26:39, 42). Discouragement is one of Satan's best ploys for bringing us down. When Jesus fasted in the desert for forty days, Satan approached Him at His weakest, hoping that He would be discouraged and thus more vulnerable to temptation. Satan was wrong that time, but he never stops trying to sabotage our faith. Billy Graham said, "Discouragement blinds our eyes to the mercy of God and makes us perceive only the unfavorable circumstances."[11]

The antidote to discouragement is encouragement. Encouragement is speaking hope into the present about the future.

"Have I not commanded you? Be strong and courageous. Do not be terrified; do not be discouraged, for the Lord your God will be with you wherever you go." Joshua 1:9

8. According to Joshua 1:9, why should we not be discouraged?

"Then you will have success if you are careful to observe the decrees and laws that the Lord gave Moses for Israel. Be strong and courageous. Do not be afraid or discouraged." 1 Chronicles 22:13

"David also said to Solomon his son, 'Be strong and courageous, and do the work. Do not be afraid or discouraged, for the Lord God, my God, is with you. He will not fail you or forsake you until all the work for the service of the temple of the Lord is finished.'" 1 Chronicles 28:20

9. What did David tell his son Solomon about discouragement in these two passages?

10. According to 1 Chronicles 28:20, why was Solomon not to be discouraged?

11. Ruth Myers said, "Discouragement often precedes enlargement."[12] What does that mean to you?

Depression

I personally feel that if you haven't dealt with depression, you haven't lived long enough. The Psalms have much to say about depression. King Saul was tormented by what many believe was depression. (See 1 Samuel 16:14-23.) Although young David played the harp to soothe the king, David himself was often plagued with bouts of depression in his later years. Many of his psalms reflect these mental and emotional struggles.

Like discouragement, depression often results when we turn our eyes away from God and others and, instead, focus on ourselves.

12. Do you have a favorite Psalm, one you turn to during times of depression? Write down an especially meaningful verse.

Despair

When you lose hope, you gain despair. Despair is the absence of hope. Despair is not believing or trusting that God can work all things for good (Romans 8:28). Read what some have said about this debilitating condition:

- "The knowledge of God without that of man's misery causes pride. The knowledge of man's misery without that of God causes despair."[13] Pascal

- "The essence of despair is relegating God solely to the past."[14] John Claypool

- "There are no hopeless situations, only people who have grown hopeless about them."[15] Charles Swindoll

13. What do you think John Claypool meant by saying that the "essence of despair is relegating God solely to the past"?

> *"We are hard pressed on every side, but not crushed; perplexed, but not in despair; persecuted, but not abandoned; struck down, but not destroyed."*
> 2 Corinthians 4:8-9

14. What did Paul say about despair in 2 Corinthians 4:8-9?

Sadness

It is perfectly natural to be sad at different times in our lives. If we never felt sadness, we would never fully comprehend the blessing of joy. Ecclesiastes 3:1-8 captures the essence of the contrasting "seasons" in our lives: *"a time to weep and a time to laugh, a time to mourn and a time to dance"* (verse 4). In "Ode to the West Wind," Shelley points to the burden of one in "sore need," a "heavy weight of hours [that] has chained and bowed One too like thee." He ends this moving poem with these powerful words of hope: "If Winter comes, can Spring be far behind?"

15. Read Psalms 6, 13, and 42.

a. Describe the physical and emotional effects of sadness as portrayed in these psalms.

b. Does the psalmist give up on God?

"The Lord is close to the brokenhearted and saves those who are crushed in spirit."
Psalm 34:18

16. How does Psalm 34:18 give you hope?

Anger

This is an emotion that may sideswipe you, knock you off balance, blindside you. You don't expect to be angry at the one who just died, but often anger is exactly what you feel. You might be angry about the circumstances surrounding your loved one's death. You might be angry at the helplessness of your situation. I have discovered that incapacity not only is frustrating, but it can lead to agitation, which can possibly lead to anger. When my friend Carolyn James described anger in her book, *When Life and Belief Collide*, she said it was "a symptom not of how wrong God has gotten things but of our need to know Him better."[16]

"Refrain from anger and turn from wrath; do not fret—it leads only to evil."
Psalm 37:8

"In your anger do not sin . . ." Ephesians 4:26a

"Do not let the sun go down while you are still angry . . ." Ephesians 4:26b

17. What do these verses reveal about anger?

a. Psalm 37:8

b. Ephesians 4:26a

18. According to Ephesians 4:26b, what is the deadline for anger?

"Bear with each other and forgive whatever grievances you may have against one another. Forgive as the Lord forgave you." Colossians 3:13

" 'Forgive us our debts, as we also have forgiven our debtors.' " Matthew 6:12

"For if you forgive men when they sin against you, your heavenly Father will also forgive you. But if you do not forgive men their sins, your Father will not forgive your sins." Matthew 6:14-15

19. According to Colossians 3:13 and Matthew 6:12, 14-15, what is the remedy for anger?

Anxiousness or Anxiety

The great English theologian F. B. Meyer said, "The word anxiety comes from the same root as anger, and suggests the idea of choking. Worry chokes the life of faith. It does not help us to overcome our difficulties, but unfits us for dealing with them."[17] Anxiety incapacitates. It feeds on the failures and missed opportunities of the past. It focuses on the "what ifs" of the future. In this way it keeps you from dealing with the present, essentially paralyzing you. Read these quotes about anxiety and then read what the Bible has to say.

- "Where faith begins, anxiety ends; where anxiety begins, faith ends."[18] George Müller, who ran his orphanage in England upon faith.

- "Anxiety is unbelief in the gracious provinces of God."[19] John Piper

- "Anxiety and prayer are two great opposing forces in Christian experience."[20]

  "Do not be anxious about anything, but in everything, by prayer and petition, with thanksgiving, present your requests to God." Philippians 4:6

  "An anxious heart weighs a man down, but a kind word cheers him up." Proverbs 12:25

20. What can you learn about anxiety from these verses?

   a. Philippians 4:6

   b. Proverbs 12:25

21. What is the remedy to anxiety, according to Philippians 4:6?

22. How can you pray with thanksgiving in everything when you are in a state of anxiety?

Worry

Worry has been called one of Satan's most effective weapons against God's peace. Max Lucado points to the Greek origin of the word worry, explaining that it means "to tear at one's mind. When the focus is on yourself, you worry."[21] Worry is another subject about which many people have something to say:

- "What worries you, masters you." Haddon W. Robinson

- "Worry does not empty tomorrow of its sorrow, it empties today of its strength." Corrie ten Boom

- "All our fret and worry is caused by calculating without God."[22] Oswald Chambers

- "Worry is like a rocking chair. It will give you something to do, but it will not take you anywhere." Skip Heitzig

   "Surely he will never be shaken; a righteous man will be remembered forever. He will have no fear of bad news; his heart is steadfast, trusting in the Lord. His heart is secure, he will have no fear; in the end he will look in triumph on his foes." Psalm 112:6-8

   "[1] Do not fret because of evil men or be envious of those who do wrong . . . [7] Be still before the Lord and wait patiently for him; do not fret when men succeed in their ways, when they carry out their wicked schemes. [8] Refrain from anger and turn from wrath; do not fret—it leads only to evil." Psalm 37:1, 7, 8

   "Cast all your anxiety on him because he cares for you." 1 Peter 5:7

23. What do these verses say about worry/fret? What remedy do they offer?

   a. Psalm 112:6-8

   b. Psalm 37:1, 7, 8

   c. 1 Peter 5:7

" 'Martha, Martha,' the Lord answered, 'you are worried and upset about many things, but only one thing is needed. Mary has chosen what is better, and it will not be taken away from her.' " Luke 10:41-42

24. What can you learn from Martha's worrying in Luke 10:41-42?

"Therefore I tell you, do not worry about your life, what you will eat or drink; or about your body, what you will wear. Is not life more important than food, and the body more important than clothes? Look at the birds of the air; they do not sow or reap or store away in barns, and yet your heavenly Father feeds them. Are you not much more valuable than they? Who of you by worrying can add a single hour to his life? And why do you worry about clothes? See how the lilies of the field grow. They do not labor or spin. Yet I tell you that not even Solomon in all his splendor was dressed like one of these. If that is how God clothes the grass of the field, which is here today and tomorrow is thrown into the fire, will he not much more clothe you, O you of little faith? So do not worry, saying, 'What shall we eat?' or 'What shall we drink?' or 'What shall we wear?' For the pagans run after all these things, and your heavenly Father knows that you need them. But seek first his kingdom and his righteousness, and all these things will be given to you as well. Therefore do not worry about tomorrow, for tomorrow will worry about itself. Each day has enough trouble of its own." Matthew 6:25-34

"Do not be afraid of those who kill the body but cannot kill the soul. Rather, be afraid of the One who can destroy both soul and body in hell. Are not two sparrows sold for a penny? Yet not one of them will fall to the ground apart from the will of your Father. And even the very hairs of your head are all numbered. So don't be afraid; you are worth more than many sparrows." Matthew 10:28-31

"Whenever you are arrested and brought to trial, do not worry beforehand about what to say. Just say whatever is given you at the time, for it is not you speaking, but the Holy Spirit." Mark 13:11

"I have told you these things, so that in me you may have peace. In this world you will have trouble. But take heart! I have overcome the world." John 16:33

25. What did Jesus say about worrying in the above verses?

   a. Matthew 6:25-34

   b. Matthew 10:28-31

   c. Mark 13:11

   d. John 16:33

> "Fear to fear. Be afraid to be afraid. Your worst enemy is within your own bosom."
>
> **C. H. Spurgeon**

Fear

I know you're afraid. Fear is a great predator. It stalks us, corners us, overwhelms us, and pierces us to the marrow. No one has ever escaped fear, not even Jesus, who was *"overwhelmed with sorrow to the point of death"* (Matthew 26: 37); *"being in anguish, he prayed more earnestly, and his sweat was like drops of blood falling to the ground"* (Luke 22:44). But Jesus arose from His knees and faced Calvary. In the same way, we must face our fears, along with the full torrent of feelings in our raging river of emotions. The surest way to address your ever-changing emotions is with the unchanging truths of Scripture.

> *"Even though I walk through the valley of the shadow of death, I will fear no evil, for you are with me; your rod and your staff, they comfort me."* Psalm 23:4

26. How did David react to fear in Psalm 23:4?

> *"Do not be afraid, little flock, for your Father has been pleased to give you the kingdom."* Luke 12:32

27. What did Jesus say about fear in Luke 12:32?

My brother Skip used to quote this one to me:

> *"For God did not give us a spirit of timidity, but a spirit of power, of love and of self-discipline."* 2 Timothy 1:7

28. According to 2 Timothy 1:7, does God give us fear?

> "Fear is a self-imposed prison that will keep you from becoming what God intends for you to be."
>
> **Rick Warren**

Confusion

Asking God "Why?" is a natural reflex. A lot of people do. This question is repeated many times in the Bible. The book of Job is full of questions. Yet, many people in pain turn to this book for answers—primarily because God did not answer the "why" questions as Job expected. He answered with His presence. His presence is the answer. This answer satisfied Job. Will it satisfy you?

> *"Why are you downcast, O my soul? Why so disturbed within me? Put your hope in God, for I will yet praise him, my Savior and my God."* Psalm 42:5

"You are my God my stronghold. Why have you rejected me?" Psalm 43:2

"Shall we accept good from God, and not trouble?" Job 2:10b

"Though he slay me, yet will I hope in him . . ." Job 13:15a

29. What do you learn from these verses that can help you through your difficult times?

30. Dawn Hall, a young widow of thirty-nine, said, "He's [God] not accountable to me; I'm accountable to Him."[23] What do you think of her statement?

SUMMARY

As a man, Jesus felt many of the emotions we feel. As God, He understands us from the inside out because He knew fear and sadness and pain when He walked among us. We also know that we can come to Him at any time—day or night, at work, in the car, dressed up for church or slogging around in sweatpants and T-shirt at home. We can come to Him and "cast all our anxiety on Him, because He cares for us."

Do the emotions we have discussed in this chapter run the gamut of what you are feeling? Feelings are real. God created us to have feelings. Our emotions are part of what distinguishes us from the rest of creation. But His truth is reality. Our challenge is to learn to live by truth (reality) and not by feelings. Feelings are like clothes, and we all know that clothes don't make the person. Emotions may mark us as human beings, but learning to control them is what marks us as mature adults.

"Perseverance must finish its work so that you may
be mature and complete, not lacking anything."
James 1:4

CHAPTER 6

GRIEVING

"To him who overcomes, I will give the right to eat from the tree of life, which is in the paradise of God."
Revelation 2:7

INTRODUCTION

Grieving will come over you like a pall. [A **pall** is a cloth which covers a casket at funerals. The word comes from the Latin *pallium* (cloak) through the Old English.] It will seem to suffocate you. One of the first responses, in fact, is an apparent lack of breath. It feels as if the breath of life has departed from you as well as from your loved one. Wally Amos of Famous Amos Cookies says, "Grieving is a very emotional reaction that overwhelms us."[1]

You will feel overwhelmed because you *are* overwhelmed. The shock of death can be overpowering. The flood of emotions can be devastating, exhausting you to the core of your being.

THINKING IT OVER

1. How long should someone grieve?

2. Does grieving have a positive side?

3. How do you work through your grief?

"Given a choice between grief and nothing, I'd choose grief."

William Faulkner

THINKING IN DEPTH

This chapter will look at four aspects of grieving: 1) the universality of grief; 2) the tears of grief; 3) the processing of grief; and 4) the uniqueness of grief. The Bible is stained with the tears of sorrow, and so we shall turn to Scripture often to look at this process of grief.

The Universality of Grief

The Shiva Foundation Web site offered this comment on grief: "Grieving asks everything of us."[2] By asking everything, it seems that grieving asks too much of us. Grieving is bearing a burden too heavy, a loss too great. Grieving is painful. But everyone at some point in time will grieve. No one in history ever has escaped the school of grief, sorrow, and pain.

- Grieving is normal.

- Grieving is emotional.

- Grieving is slow.

- Grieving is ongoing.

One of the reasons grief is painful is the realization that we are not in control; the clock wasn't ours to wind. John Claypool explains, "Grief comes back to this: We ran out of time. Something ends before we want it to."[3]

How true his words are. Is this not indicative of someone intimate with pain? Read these quotes on grief and see if you can identify with some of the thoughts.

- "There's no greater grief than remembering happier times." Dante

- "The widow mourns twice: once for your spouse and again for the life you used to live together."[4]

- "Unresolved grief is almost always about undelivered communications."[5] The Grief Recovery Institute

- "Grief is both a painful necessity and a privilege, for it comes as a result of having loved."[6] Alan D. Wolfelt

1. In *Much Ado About Nothing*, Shakespeare wrote, "Everyone can master a grief but he that has it." What do you think he meant by that statement?

"Grief is the price we pay for love."

Queen Elizabeth II

"Though he brings grief, he will show compassion, so great is his unfailing love. For he does not willingly bring affliction or grief to the children of men." Lamentations 3:32-33

2. What do you learn from Lamentations 3:32-33?

"The heart of the wise is in the house of mourning, but the heart of fools is in the house of pleasure." Ecclesiastes 7:4

3. According to Ecclesiastes 7:4, who grieves—the wise or the foolish?

The Tears of Grief

I don't know how you feel about crying. For most people, crying comes naturally when they experience loss. Some people do not cry. Personally, I think there is a blessing to be gained from tears. Luke 6:21b tells us, *"Blessed are you who weep now, for you will laugh."* Crying is also a way to cleanse the spirit: *" 'Even now,' declares the Lord, 'return to me with all your heart, with fasting and weeping and mourning.' Rend your heart and not your garments. Return to the Lord your God, for he is gracious and compassionate, slow to anger and abounding in love, and he relents from sending calamity"* (Joel 2:12-13).

Dr. Thomas Frantz, a professor and an authority on bereavement counseling, says crying is the most natural way to release grief. (Ironically, he notes that the first goal for most people is to get the grieving person to stop crying!) Tears are natural. Babies come into the world crying. Did you know that tears of grief contain more toxins than normal tears? They are cleansing and healing! In *Oliver Twist*, Charles Dickens said that crying "opens the lungs, washes the countenance, exercises the eyes, and softens down the temper."

The Bible includes many examples of criers (not crybabies!):

"She died at Kiriath Arba (that is, Hebron) in the land of Canaan, and Abraham went to mourn for Sarah and to weep over her." Genesis 23:2 [Abraham mourning the death of his wife]

"Deeply moved at the sight of his brother, Joseph hurried out and looked for a place to weep. He went into his private room and wept there." Genesis 43:30 [Joseph, seeing his brother for the first time since he had been taken to Egypt]

Elkanah her husband would say to her, 'Hannah, why are you weeping? Why don't you eat? Why are you downhearted? Don't I mean more to you than ten sons?' " 1 Samuel 1:8 [Hannah, distraught over her childlessness]

"Grief is like a long . . . winding valley, where any bend may reveal a totally new landscape."

C. S. Lewis

"So David and his men wept aloud until they had no strength left to weep." 1 Samuel 30:4 [David, at the destruction of Ziklag]

"But David continued up the Mount of Olives, weeping as he went; his head was covered and he was barefoot. All the people with him covered their heads too and were weeping as they went up." 2 Samuel 15:30 [David, departing Jerusalem after his son's betrayal]

"Oh, that my head were a spring of water and my eyes a fountain of tears! I would weep day and night for the slain of my people." Jeremiah 9:1 [the prophet Jeremiah speaking]

"But if you do not listen, I will weep in secret because of your pride; my eyes will weep bitterly, overflowing with tears, because the Lord's flock will be taken captive." Jeremiah 13:17 [the prophet Jeremiah speaking]

"Speak this word to them: 'Let my eyes overflow with tears night and day without ceasing; for my virgin daughter—my people—has suffered a grievous wound, a crushing blow.' " Jeremiah 14:17 [the prophet Jeremiah speaking]

"My face is red with weeping, deep shadows ring my eyes . . . My intercessor is my friend as my eyes pour out tears to God." Job 16:16, 20 [Job speaking]

"Have I not wept for those in trouble? Has not my soul grieved for the poor?" Job 30:25 [Job speaking]

"I served the Lord with great humility and with tears, although I was severely tested by the plots of the Jews . . . So be on your guard! Remember that for three years I never stopped warning each of you night and day with tears." Acts 20:19, 31 [the apostle Paul speaking]

"For, as I have often told you before and now say again even with tears, many live as enemies of the cross of Christ." Philippians 3:18 [the apostle Paul speaking]

"Recalling your tears, I long to see you, so that I may be filled with joy." 2 Timothy 1:4 [Paul speaking of Timothy's tears]

"And as she stood behind him at his feet weeping, she began to wet his feet with her tears. Then she wiped them with her hair, kissed them and poured perfume on them." Luke 7:38 [referring to a sinful woman]

"Then the disciples went back to their homes, but Mary stood outside the tomb crying. As she wept, she bent over to look into the tomb and saw two angels in white, seated where Jesus' body had been, one at the head and the other at the foot. They asked her, 'Woman, why are you crying?' 'They have taken my Lord away,' she said, 'and I don't know where they have put him.' At this, she turned around and saw Jesus standing there, but she did not realize that it was Jesus. 'Woman,' he said, 'why are you crying? Who is it you are looking for?' " John 20:10-14 [referring to Mary Magdalene]

"Jesus wept." John 11:35 [Jesus outside the tomb of Lazarus]

"When Jesus saw her weeping, and the Jews who had come along with her also weeping, he was deeply moved in spirit and troubled." John 11:33 [Jesus reacting to Mary's grief and tears]

In the following Scriptures, let's delve more deeply into the subject of tears:

"[There is] a time to weep and a time to laugh." Ecclesiastes 3:4

"Weeping may remain for a night, but rejoicing comes in the morning." Psalm 30:5b

4. What do we learn about weeping/crying from Ecclesiastes 3:4 and Psalm 30:5b?

"I am worn out from groaning; all night long I flood my bed with weeping and drench my couch with tears." Psalm 6:6

"Streams of tears flow from my eyes because my people are destroyed. My eyes will flow unceasingly, without relief, until the Lord looks down from heaven and sees." Lamentations 3:48-51

"This is why I weep and my eyes overflow with tears. No one is near to comfort me, no one to restore my spirit." Lamentations 1:16

5. From these three Scriptures, describe some of the feelings associated with crying/weeping.

"The cords of death entangled me, the anguish of the grave came upon me; I was overcome by trouble and sorrow. Then I called on the name of the Lord: 'O Lord, save me!' . . . For you, O Lord, have delivered my soul from death, my eyes from tears, my feet from stumbling." Psalm 116:3-4, 8

6. What does God do for those who call on His name in times of trouble and sorrow?

"Those who sow in tears will reap with songs of joy." Psalm 126:5

7. What do you think the psalmist means by "sow in tears" in Psalm 126:5?

"My tears have been my food day and night . . ." Psalm 42:3a

"You have fed them with the bread of tears; you have made them drink tears by the bowlful." Psalm 80:5

8. To what are tears compared in Psalms 42:3a and 80:5?

"Go back and tell Hezekiah, the leader of my people, 'This is what the Lord, the God of your father David, says: "I have heard your prayer and seen your tears; I will heal you." ' " 2 Kings 20:5a [See also Isaiah 38:5.]

"Away from me, all you who do evil, for the Lord has heard my weeping." Psalm 6:8

"Record my lament; list my tears on your scroll—are they not in your record?" Psalm 56:8

9. Regarding tears, what do we learn about God from these Scriptures?

    a. 2 Kings 20:5a

    b. Psalm 6:8

    c. Psalm 56:8

"He will swallow up death forever. The Sovereign Lord will wipe away the tears from all faces . . ." Isaiah 25:8a

"He will lead them to springs of living water. And God will wipe away every tear from their eyes." Revelation 7:17b, c

"He will wipe every tear from their eyes. There will be no more death or mourning or crying or pain, for the old order of things has passed away." Revelation 21:4

10. What do these three Scriptures tell us God will do about our crying?

The Processing of Grief

In dealing with our emotions, we have learned that while we all experience such feelings as anger, sadness, and worry, we experience them at different intensities and duration. Since we are all unique, the way we grieve is also unique. We experience grief in different degrees and we process grief in different ways.

Process is probably the best way to describe grieving. It involves differing, cloudy stages through which we pass. Some of these stages include:

denial   Depression   **alarm**

Anger   Desperation/Distress

RESENTMENT   CONFUSION/FRUSTRATION

guilt   *numbness*

SHOCK   ACCEPTANCE/RESIGNATION

Bargaining   LONELINESS/ISOLATION

> "Like a raging fire, grief has its way."
>
> **Paula D'Arcy**

On Death and Dying is a groundbreaking study of grief that is still used as a reference in many psychology courses. Author Elisabeth Kübler-Ross, M.D. identifies five primary stages in the grieving process: denial, anger, bargaining, depression, and acceptance.[7] She arranges these progressively; in other words, the one grieving should eventually move from denial to acceptance. There are all sorts of possible "stops" or "detours" along the way.

In *Shattered Dreams*, Larry Crabb says, "Grief can only be embraced, never managed."[8] During my grieving experience, I felt that grief could only be endured, not embraced. I experienced more stages than the Kübler-Ross model. The stages or steps are not exact or determined. You may enter at any level and go in any direction. For example, if your loved one suffered a lengthy debilitating illness before he died, you may not experience the shock of death as intensely as another woman who loses her husband unexpectedly.

Having gone through one level doesn't necessarily mean that you are through with that level. You may visit different stages all within an hour—or a minute! You may repeat certain stages again and again, or completely bypass others. Grief is fluid, ever changing, ever flowing. It is a process. Dr. Thomas Frantz explains grief as "a form of energy we have to learn to expend."[9] He describes it as a process through which we release the negative energy we have taken in.

One stage may involve doubting God. You are not the first to do so. I mention Job so often because he is an example of someone who questioned the circumstances of his life, but never abandoned his faith in God. He dared to ask "Why?" without ever losing hope. You can do the same. Take your doubts and questions to God. Job did and God honored him. That is what distinguishes those who mourn without faith from Christians.

I was told of a woman who had lost her husband tragically. She was an atheist, as was her husband. There was no funeral because they had decided earlier not to conduct rites of any kind after their deaths. She was devastated by his death, but could not be comforted. When someone asked me to visit this widow, I responded, "How can I comfort someone who will not accept the only hope that I know?" For without the promise of eternal life through Jesus Christ, there is no hope. There is only desperation. Words without a message of hope are empty words—they cannot comfort.

> "[13] Brothers, we do not want you to be ignorant about those who fall asleep, or to grieve like the rest of men, who have no hope. [14] We believe that Jesus died and rose again and so we believe that God will bring with Jesus those who have fallen asleep in him. [15] According to the Lord's own word, we tell you that we who are still alive, who are left till the coming of the Lord, will certainly not precede those who have fallen asleep. [16] For the Lord himself will come down from heaven, with a loud command, with the voice of the archangel and with the trumpet call of God, and the dead in Christ will rise first. [17] After that, we who are still alive and are left will be caught up together with them in the clouds to meet the Lord in the air. And so we will be with the Lord forever. [18] Therefore encourage each other with these words." 1 Thessalonians 4:13-18

11. According to this passage, do Christians grieve differently? Why?

12. What does 1 Thessalonians 4:18 tell us to do?

13. How do you process your pain or make sense of it all?

14. How is grieving draining you?

15. What can you do to reenergize yourself?

"Nehemiah said, 'Go and enjoy choice food and sweet drinks, and send some to those who have nothing prepared. This day is sacred to our Lord. Do not grieve, for the joy of the Lord is your strength.'" Nehemiah 8:10

16. How do we find strength in grieving, according to Nehemiah 8:10? (Note: We will look at this subject in more depth in Chapters 7 and 8.)

"Therefore we do not lose heart. Though outwardly we are wasting away, yet inwardly we are being renewed day by day. For our light and momentary troubles are achieving for us an eternal glory that far outweighs them all. So we fix our eyes not on what is seen, but on what is unseen. For what is seen is temporary, but what is unseen is eternal." 2 Corinthians 4:16-18

17. According to 2 Corinthians 4:16-18, why do we not lose heart?

"Godly sorrow brings repentance that leads to salvation and leaves no regret, but worldly sorrow brings death." 2 Corinthians 7:10

18. According to 2 Corinthians 7:10, does godly sorrow have regrets?

> "Grief changes everything and everyone."
>
> **Paula D'Arcy**

The Uniqueness of Grief

Your grief is yours alone. You cannot delegate it to someone else. It will not be the same, and you will not be the same. Although I was widowed along with three other women, we all felt the same loss: the sudden, unexpected death of a spouse. We were very much alike and had a lot in common—most significantly, our hope in Christ. However, we all processed this loss differently. Nearly two years later, we were all at different stages. We understood that we were different people coping the best way we knew how. We gave each other room to be ourselves and to grieve in the way that fit us best.

Please give your widowed friends room to grieve in the way that best facilitates their grieving process, even if it differs from the way you process your grief. And give yourself room to process your own grief. My friend Debbie calls this her "grief work." She is spending time and energy on working through her grief. Sometimes, it's just crying through it. You won't even know what your own needs are at first, much less the needs of others. Allow yourself and those around you the space to breathe and adjust. That's something I never realized until this "happened to me."

SUMMARY

Grieving is not just about you. You are not an island in this process (even though you may feel that way). This impacted you personally, yes, but it impacted so many others too. You not only will need to process your own grief, but also help those around you process theirs (while respecting their boundaries, as well). You may find yourself becoming much like a confessor. That has happened to me; people come to tell me their feelings about their loved ones—both good and bad.

Taking time to grieve may seem selfish. But, it is not. It is a very generous process. You are sharing yourself and your loss with others—at times, whether you want to or not!

In this process of grieving for her missionary husband, Mrs. Charles Cowman wrote, "Sorrow is God's plowshare that turns up and subsoils the depths of the soul, that it may yield richer harvests . . . Hence, it is sorrow that makes us think deeply, long, and soberly. Sorrow makes us go slower and more considerately . . . It takes sorrow to widen the soul."[10]

> *"Sorrow is better than laughter: for by the sadness*
> *of the countenance the heart is made better."*
> Ecclesiastes 7:3 KJV

"Love doesn't stop at death . . . Grief could almost be defined as the form love takes when the object of love has been removed; it is love embracing an empty space, love kissing thin air and feeling the pain of nothingness."

N. T. Wright

CHAPTER 7

COPING

"The eternal God is your refuge, and underneath are the everlasting arms."
Deuteronomy 33:27a

INTRODUCTION

If grieving is an ongoing process, then the need to cope will be constant. How do you cope? How do you go on? People will offer all kinds of "helpful" and often contradictory advice: stay busy; don't do too much too quickly; "bury yourself" in your work, your children, your church; free yourself from too many commitments. It's all very confusing.

Fellow widow Elisabeth Elliot followed her mother's advice. Quoting an old poem, Elisabeth's mother often said: "Just do the next thing."[1] That phrase has become a watchword for Elisabeth. Coach Bill Parcells took this one step further. He said, "Do the right thing." Doing the next thing and the right thing are important. However, I think the best thing you can do is to read God's Word and speak God's truth. Read God's truth. Learn the truth. Digest the truth—the real, eternal, unchanging, great Truth versus the daily, changing, discouraging, lesser truths. Then, remind yourself of God's truths. Preach them to yourself! This is critically important because the world inundates you every day with its lesser truths through TV, radio, film, newspapers, and even well-meaning friends.

THINKING IT OVER

1. What helps you get through your days?

2. What is the best thing someone has said or done to help you cope in this process?

3. What is the one thing you wish people knew that would help you cope? Can you tell them?

THINKING IN DEPTH

Coping is like weathering a storm. When you encounter inclement weather, you generally take the following steps:

- Retreat or take shelter.
- Be patient as you wait for the storm to pass.
- Acknowledge that you are not in control.
- Occupy yourself with productive things to do while you wait.
- Prepare to "go out" again when the storm subsides.

Mrs. Charles Cowman said, "Jesus Christ is no security against storms, but He is perfect security in storms. He has never promised you an easy passage, only a safe landing."[2] In this chapter, we will examine several aspects of God's truth to help you see that you are always secure in Christ during any of life's storms. (In the next two chapters, we will look at specific ways to cope.)

"I praise you because I am fearfully and wonderfully made; your works are wonderful, I know that full well." Psalm 139:14

"Your eyes saw my unformed body. All the days ordained for me were written in your book before one of them came to be." Psalm 139:16

"I know, O Lord, that a man's life is not his own; it is not for man to direct his steps." Jeremiah 10:23

"In his heart a man plans his course, but the Lord determines his steps." Proverbs 16:9

"A man's steps are directed by the Lord. How then can anyone understand his own way?" Proverbs 20:24

"This man was handed over to you by God's set purpose and foreknowledge . . ." Acts 2:23

"They did what your power and will had decided beforehand should happen." Acts 4:28

"I cry out to God Most High, to God, who fulfills his purpose for me." Psalm 57:2

"The Lord will fulfill his purpose for me; your love, O Lord, endures forever—do not abandon the works of your hands." Psalm 138:8

". . .who has saved us and called us to a holy life—not because of anything we have done but because of his own purpose and grace. This grace was given us in Christ Jesus before the beginning of time . . ." 2 Timothy 1:9

1. What great truths do you see in these verses?

    a. Psalm 139:14

    b. Psalm 139:16

    c. Jeremiah 10:23

    d. Proverbs 16:9

    e. Proverbs 20:24

    f. Acts 2:23 and 4:28

    g. Psalms 57:2 and 138:8

    h. 2 Timothy 1:9

2. How would you summarize what these verses tell us?

"A deep distress hath humanised my Soul."

William Wordsworth

The truths I have found to be the most comforting to me, those that have helped me to cope are these:

- God hears.
- God knows.
- God cares.
- God is good.
- God loves.
- God is with you.
- God is in you.
- God plans.
- God sustains.

These are truths we need to repeat over and over—truths we need to preach to ourselves:

I. GOD HEARS

> *"The angel of the Lord found Hagar near a spring in the desert; it was the spring that is beside the road to Shur. And he said, 'Hagar, servant of Sarai, where have you come from, and where are you going?' 'I'm running away from my mistress Sarai,' she answered. Then the angel of the Lord told her, 'Go back to your mistress and submit to her.' The angel added, 'I will so increase your descendants that they will be too numerous to count.' The angel of the Lord also said to her: 'You are now with child and you will have a son. You shall name him Ishmael, for the Lord has heard of your misery.'"* Genesis 16:7-11

> *"And Abraham said to God, 'If only Ishmael might live under your blessing!' Then God said, 'Yes, but your wife Sarah will bear you a son, and you will call him Isaac. I will establish my covenant with him as an everlasting covenant for his descendants after him. And as for Ishmael, I have heard you: I will surely bless him; I will make him fruitful and will greatly increase his numbers. He will be the father of twelve rulers, and I will make him into a great nation.'"* Genesis 17:18-20

> *"God heard the boy [Ishmael] crying, and the angel of God called to Hagar from heaven and said to her, 'What is the matter, Hagar? Do not be afraid; God has heard the boy crying as he lies there. Lift the boy up and take him by the hand, for I will make him into a great nation.' Then God opened her eyes and she saw a well of water. So she went and filled the skin with water and gave the boy a drink. God was with the boy as he grew up. He lived in the desert and became an archer."* Genesis 21:17-20

> *"Isaac prayed to the Lord on behalf of his wife, because she was barren. The Lord answered his prayer, and his wife Rebekah became pregnant."* Genesis 25:21

> *"Then God remembered Rachel; he listened to her and opened her womb."* Genesis 30:22

"Grief is a crisis that requires a person to work out new ways of coping."

Stephen Ministries

3. List the people God heard in these Scriptures from **Genesis**.

    a. 16:7-11

    b. 17:18-20

    c. 21:17-20

    d. 25:21

    e. 30:22

The Psalms also offer many examples of how God hears us.

"To the Lord I cry aloud, and he answers me from his holy hill." Psalm 3:4

"Answer me when I call to you, O my righteous God. Give me relief from my distress; be merciful to me and hear my prayer." Psalm 4:1

"Know that the Lord has set apart the godly for himself; the Lord will hear when I call to him." Psalm 4:3

"Away from me, all you who do evil, for the Lord has heard my weeping. The Lord has heard my cry for mercy; the Lord accepts my prayer." Psalm 6:8, 9

"For he who avenges blood remembers; he does not ignore the cry of the afflicted." Psalm 9:12

"You hear, O Lord, the desire of the afflicted; you encourage them, and you listen to their cry." Psalm 10:17

"In my distress I called to the Lord; I cried to my God for help. From his temple he heard my voice; my cry came before him, into his ears." Psalm 18:6

"For he has not despised or disdained the suffering of the afflicted one; he has not hidden his face from him but has listened to his cry for help." Psalm 22:24

"Praise be to the Lord, for he has heard my cry for mercy." Psalm 28:6

"In my alarm I said, 'I am cut off from your sight!' Yet you heard my cry for mercy when I called to you for help." Psalm 31:22

"I waited patiently for the Lord; he turned to me and heard my cry." Psalm 40:1

"Evening, morning and noon I cry out in distress, and he hears my voice." Psalm 55:17

"But God has surely listened and heard my voice in prayer." Psalm 66:19

"Hear my prayer, O Lord; listen to my cry for mercy. In the day of my trouble I will call to you, for you will answer me." Psalm 86:6, 7

"He will call upon me, and I will answer him; I will be with him in trouble, I will deliver him and honor him." Psalm 91:15

4. What do you learn from these verses in **Psalms**?

    a. 3:4

    b. 4:1

    c. 4:3

    d. 6:8, 9

    e. 9:12

    f. 10:17

    g. 18:6

    h. 22:24

    i. 28:6

    j. 31:22

    k. 40:1

    l. 55:17

    m. 66:19

    n. 86:6, 7

    o. 91:15

5. What comfort do you find in the above verses?

"The Lord is near to all who call on him, to all who call on him in truth."
Psalm 145:18

"Then you will call upon me and come and pray to me, and I will listen to you. You will seek me and find me when you seek me with all your heart." Jeremiah 29:12, 13

"This is the confidence we have in approaching God: that if we ask anything according to his will, he hears us." 1 John 5:14

"We know that God does not listen to sinners. He listens to the godly man who does his will." John 9:31

6. What requirements does God place on those who call on Him?

a. Psalm 145:18

b. Jeremiah 29:12, 13

c. 1 John 5:14

d. John 9:31

II. GOD KNOWS

"[1] O Lord, you have searched me and you know me. [2] You know when I sit and when I rise; you perceive my thoughts from afar. [3] You discern my going out and my lying down; you are familiar with all my ways. [4] Before a word is on my tongue you know it completely, O Lord. [5] You hem me in—behind and before; you have laid your hand upon me. [6] Such knowledge is too wonderful for me, too lofty for me to attain." Psalm 139:1-6

7. What do we learn about God from Psalm 139:1-6?

a. verse 1

b. verse 2

c. verse 3

d. verse 4

e. verse 5

f. verse 6

"Would not God have discovered it, since he knows the secrets of the heart?"
Psalm 44:21

"Does he not see my ways and count my every step?" Job 31:4

8. What do we learn about God in these two verses?

a. Psalm 44:21

b. Job 31:4

III. GOD CARES

"I, the Lord, have called you in righteousness; I will take hold of your hand. I will keep you and will make you to be a covenant for the people and a light for the Gentiles . . ." Isaiah 42:6

"And the peace of God, which transcends all understanding, will guard your hearts and your minds in Christ Jesus." Philippians 4:7

"The Lord your God, who is going before you, will fight for you, as he did for you in Egypt, before your very eyes . . ." Deuteronomy 1:30

9. How does God show that He cares, according to these Scriptures?

a. Isaiah 42:6

b. Philippians 4:7

c. Deuteronomy 1:30

"Can a mother forget the baby at her breast and have no compassion on the child she has borne? Though she may forget, I will not forget you!" Isaiah 49:15

10. According to Isaiah 49:15, has God forgotten about you?

"You did not choose me, but I chose you and appointed you to go and bear fruit—fruit that will last. Then the Father will give you whatever you ask in my name." John 15:16

"I wish that all men were as I am. But each man has his own gift from God; one has this gift, another has that." 1 Corinthians 7:7

"But to each one of us grace has been given as Christ apportioned it. This is why it says: 'When he ascended on high, he led captives in his train and gave gifts to men.' (What does 'he ascended' mean except that he also descended to the lower, earthly regions? He who descended is the very one who ascended higher than all the heavens, in order to fill the whole universe.) It was he who gave some to be apostles, some to be prophets, some to be evangelists, and some to be pastors and teachers, to prepare God's people for works of service, so that the body of Christ may be built up until we all reach unity in the faith and in the knowledge of the Son of God and become mature, attaining to the whole measure of the fullness of Christ. Then we will no longer be infants, tossed back and forth by the waves, and blown here and there by every wind of teaching and by the cunning and craftiness of men in their deceitful scheming." Ephesians 4:7-14

"For God so loved the world that he gave his one and only Son, that whoever believes in him shall not perish but have eternal life." John 3:16

Read Romans 14.

11. From these Scriptures, we can learn how God sees us. How does this help you?

　　a. You are chosen [John 15:16]

　　b. You are gifted [1 Corinthians 7:7 and Ephesians 4:7-14]

　　c. You are special [Romans 14]

　　d. You are loved [John 3:16]

"The eternal God is your refuge, and underneath are the everlasting arms."
Deuteronomy 33:27a

"He tends his flock like a shepherd: He gathers the lambs in his arms and carries them close to his heart; he gently leads those that have young." Isaiah 40:11

"O Jerusalem, Jerusalem, you who kill the prophets and stone those sent to you, how often I have longed to gather your children together, as a hen gathers her chicks under her wings, but you were not willing." Matthew 23:37 [See also Luke 13:34.]

12. These Scriptures give us "pictures" of God as He relates to us. What are those pictures?

    a. Deuteronomy 33:27a

    b. Isaiah 40:11

    c. Matthew 23:37

IV. God Is Good

A friend and fellow widow, Debbie, says that her twin pegs of theology, the key concepts upon which she hangs everything, are these: "God is sovereign and God is good." We will look at God's sovereignty later. Trusting in God's goodness helps you to cope in the grieving process.

"The trumpeters and singers joined in unison, as with one voice, to give praise and thanks to the Lord. Accompanied by trumpets, cymbals and other instruments, they raised their voices in praise to the Lord and sang: 'He is good; his love endures forever.' Then the temple of the Lord was filled with a cloud . . ." 2 Chronicles 5:13

13. What were the words of the song the celebrants sang in 2 Chronicles 5:13?

" 'Why do you ask me about what is good?' Jesus replied. 'There is only One who is good. If you want to enter life, obey the commandments.' " Matthew 19:17

" 'Why do you call me good?' Jesus answered. 'No one is good—except God alone.' " Mark 10:18

"For the Lord is good and his love endures forever; his faithfulness continues through all generations." Psalm 100:5

14. According to Jesus in Matthew 19:17 and Mark 10:18, who alone is good?

15. Psalm 100:5 says that God is good. How long will His love and faithfulness last?

16. How have you seen or experienced God's goodness through this trial?

V. GOD LOVES

"Then my enemies will turn back when I call for help. By this I will know that God is for me. In God, whose word I praise—in God I trust; I will not be afraid. What can man do to me?" Psalm 56:9-11

"I in them and you in me. May they be brought to complete unity to let the world know that you sent me and have loved them even as you have loved me." John 17:23 [Jesus speaking]

"Give thanks to the Lord, for he is good; his love endures forever." 1 Chronicles 16:34

17. Psalm 56:9-11 tells us that God is for _____.

18. John 17:23 tells us God loves us even as He loved _____.

19. 1 Chronicles 16:34 says His love _____.

VI. GOD IS WITH YOU

One of the most encouraging statements I heard during the bewildering period of grief was that of my friend D.J. Sometimes he would put his hand on my shoulder and simply say, "God is with you." Those words resonated long after he left. Isn't it amazing that this phrase "God is with us" begins and ends the salvation story of Matthew?

" 'The virgin will be with child and will give birth to a son, and they will call him Immanuel'—which means, 'God is with us.' " Matthew 1:23 [the first chapter]

"And teaching them to obey everything I have commanded you. And surely I am with you always, to the very end of the age." Matthew 28:20 [the last chapter]

"God is with us" serves as bookends in the book of Matthew. One widow said, "To be left alone without God would be too awful for words, but to be left alone with Him is a foretaste of heaven."[3] Thomas Watson explains, "God will be with us in trouble, not only to behold us, but to uphold us."[4]

"But a time is coming, and has come, when you will be scattered, each to his own home. You will leave me all alone. Yet I am not alone, for my Father is with me." John 16:32

20. In John 16:32, Jesus says that although the disciples will leave Him all alone, He will not be alone. Who was with Him?

"If ye love me, keep my commandments. And I will pray the Father, and he shall give you another Comforter, that he may abide with you for ever; Even the Spirit of truth." John 14:15-17a KJV

21. Who did Jesus send to us so we would not be alone, according to John 14:15-17a?

"Have I not commanded you? Be strong and courageous. Do not be terrified; do not be discouraged, for the Lord your God will be with you wherever you go." Joshua 1:9

"So do not fear, for I am with you; do not be dismayed, for I am your God. I will strengthen you and help you; I will uphold you with my righteous right hand." Isaiah 41:10

"For the Lord your God is the one who goes with you to fight for you against your enemies to give you victory." Deuteronomy 20:4

"Be strong and courageous. Do not be afraid or terrified because of them, for the Lord your God goes with you; he will never leave you nor forsake you." Deuteronomy 31:6

"The Lord replied, 'My Presence will go with you, and I will give you rest.'" Exodus 33:14

22. What did God promise the Israelites, according to these Scriptures?

    a. Joshua 1:9

    b. Isaiah 41:10

    c. Deuteronomy 20:4

    d. Deuteronomy 31:6

    e. Exodus 33:14

"But Moses said to God, 'Who am I, that I should go to Pharaoh and bring the Israelites out of Egypt?' And God said, 'I will be with you. And this will be the sign to you that it is I who have sent you: When you have brought the people out of Egypt, you will worship God on this mountain.' " Exodus 3:11-12

23. How did God reassure Moses in Exodus 3:11-12?

"Even though I walk through the valley of the shadow of death, I will fear no evil, for you are with me; your rod and your staff, they comfort me." Psalm 23:4

24. In Psalm 23:4 David describes the most frightening thing we can face.

    a. What was he certain of?

    b. What did the shepherd's symbols (the rod and staff) do for David?

"David also said to Solomon his son, 'Be strong and courageous, and do the work. Do not be afraid or discouraged, for the Lord God, my God, is with you. He will not fail you or forsake you until all the work for the service of the temple of the Lord is finished.' " 1 Chronicles 28:20

25. How did David encourage his son Solomon in 1 Chronicles 28:20?

" 'But Lord,' Gideon asked, 'how can I save Israel? My clan is the weakest in Manasseh, and I am the least in my family.' The Lord answered, 'I will be with you, and you will strike down all the Midianites together.' " Judges 6:15-16

26. How did the Lord calm Gideon's fears in Judges 6:15-16?

"The Lord your God is with you, he is mighty to save. He will take great delight in you, he will quiet you with his love, he will rejoice over you with singing." Zephaniah 3:17

27. What does Zephaniah 3:17 tell us about God and His relationship with us?

" 'But now be strong, O Zerubbabel,' declares the Lord. 'Be strong, O Joshua son of Jehozadak, the high priest. Be strong, all you people of the land,' declares the Lord, 'and work. For I am with you,' declares the Lord Almighty." Haggai 2:4

28. What two things does the Lord tell the people of the land to do in Haggai 2:4? What does He tell them He will do?

"Say to those with fearful hearts, 'Be strong, do not fear; your God will come, he will come with vengeance; with divine retribution he will come to save you.' " Isaiah 35:4

29. What did God tell Isaiah to tell those with "fearful hearts" in Isaiah 35:4?

"But by the grace of God I am what I am, and his grace to me was not without effect. No, I worked harder than all of men—yet not I, but the grace of God that was with me." 1 Corinthians 15:10

30. What encouraged Paul in 1 Corinthians 15:10?

"Keep your lives free from the love of money and be content with what you have, because God has said, 'Never will I leave you; never will I forsake you.' " Hebrews 13:5

31. What words of encouragement do you find in Hebrews 13:5?

"And surely I am with you always, to the very end of the age." Matthew 28:20b

32. What were Jesus' last words to His disciples, according to Matthew 28:20?

Even more powerful than the assurance that God is with you, is that . . .

VII. GOD IS IN YOU

Larry Crabb said, "The Bible is clear. God exists. He exists in heaven. He exists on earth. He exists everywhere. More important, He exists in us."[5]

"For it is God who works in you to will and to act according to his good purpose." Philippians 2:13

33. According to Philippians 2:13?

   a. Who works in us?

   b. To do what?

"May the God of peace, who through the blood of the eternal covenant brought back from the dead our Lord Jesus, that great Shepherd of the sheep, equip you with every thing good for doing his will, and may he work in us what is pleasing to him, through Jesus Christ, to whom be glory for ever and ever. Amen." Hebrews 13:20-21

34. According to Hebrews 13:20-21:

   a. Who works in us?

   b. Why?

"There are different kinds of working, but the same God works all of them in all men." 1 Corinthians 12:6

35. What is the common denominator in 1 Corinthians 12:6?

"No one has ever seen God; but if we love one another, God lives in us and his love is made complete in us." 1 John 4:12

36. According to 1 John 4:12?

   a. If we love, who lives in us?

   b. And what does that do to us?

   c. Does knowing that you are complete help during this time when you feel so "incomplete"?

   d. Why is it important to find your completion in the right places? What are some wrong places to look for completion?

"Those who obey his commands live in him, and he in them. And this is how we know that he lives in us: We know it by the Spirit he gave us." 1 John 3:24

37. 1 John 3:24 clarifies how we know God lives in us.

   a. What condition is laid out in 1 John 3:24?

   b. How do we know He lives in us?

38. Ravi Zacharias said, "It is not our victories that make us who we are; it is His divine presence that carries us through both victory and defeat, and defines us."[6] How can this help you?

Because He lives in us, what should we do?

Examine the following Scriptures to gain a better understanding.

"Do you not know that your body is a temple of the Holy Spirit, who is in you, whom you have received from God? You are not your own; you were bought at a price. Therefore honor God with your body." 1 Corinthians 6:19-20

"What agreement is there between the temple of God and idols? For we are the temple of the living God. As God has said: 'I will live with them and walk among them, and I will be their God, and they will be my people.'" 2 Corinthians 6:16

". . . the Spirit of truth. The world cannot accept him, because it neither sees him nor knows him. But you know him, for he lives with you and will be in you." John 14:17

"I have been crucified with Christ and I no longer live, but Christ lives in me. The life I live in the body, I live by faith in the Son of God, who loved me and gave himself for me." Galatians 2:20

39. As we think about how we should live, what light do these Scriptures bring?

    a. 1 Corinthians 6:19-20

    b. 2 Corinthians 6:16

    c. John 14:17

    d. Galatians 2:20

"[He] set his seal of ownership on us, and put his Spirit in our hearts as a deposit, guaranteeing what is to come." 2 Corinthians 1:22

40. According to 2 Corinthians 1:22, what is in our hearts?

"Let the word of Christ dwell in you richly as you teach and admonish one another with all wisdom, and as you sing psalms, hymns and spiritual songs with gratitude in your hearts to God." Colossians 3:16

41. What else should we want to have live in us, according to Colossians 3:16?

"To them God has chosen to make known among the Gentiles the glorious riches of this mystery, which is Christ in you, the hope of glory." Colossians 1:27

42. What did Paul call this in Colossians 1:27?

"I pray that out of his glorious riches he may strengthen you with power through his Spirit in your inner being, so that Christ may dwell in your hearts through faith. And I pray that you, being rooted and established in love, may have power, together with all the saints, to grasp how wide and long and high and deep is the love of Christ, and to know this love that surpasses knowledge—that you may be filled to the measure of all the fullness of God." Ephesians 3:16-19

43. What did Paul pray for in Ephesians 3:16-19?

"I have given them the glory that you gave me, that they may be one as we are one: I in them and you in me. May they be brought to complete unity to let the world know that you sent me and have loved them even as you have loved me." John 17:22-23

44. What does Jesus most desire, as reflected in His High Priestly Prayer (John 17:22-23)?

"You, however, are controlled not by the sinful nature but by the Spirit, if the Spirit of God lives in you. And if anyone does not have the Spirit of Christ, he does not belong to Christ." Romans 8:9

45. If God lives in us, what should control us, according to Romans 8:9?

46. "What God seeks in every individual is not just companionship based on His intervention, but communion with Him based on His indwelling."[7] How does this statement speak to you?

VIII. GOD PLANS

Does God have a plan for my life and your life? Right now, I know it doesn't feel that way. But read these verses and decide for yourself. *"Then you will know the truth, and the truth will set you free"* (John 8:32).

47. Write what you discover about God's plan/purpose after each verse:

"But God sent me ahead of you to preserve for you a remnant on earth and to save your lives by a great deliverance." Genesis 45:7 [Joseph speaking to his brothers in Egypt]

a.

"For if you remain silent at this time, relief and deliverance for the Jews will arise from another place, but you and your father's family will perish. And who knows but that you have come to royal position for such a time as this?" Esther 4:14 [Mordecai to Esther]

b.

"If the Lord delights in a man's way, he makes his steps firm." Psalm 37:23

"The law of his God is in his heart; his feet do not slip." Psalm 37:31

c.

"I cry out to God Most High, to God, who fulfills his purpose for me." Psalm 57:2

d.

"The Lord will fulfill his purpose for me; your love, O Lord, endures forever—do not abandon the works of your hands." Psalm 138:8

e.

"He carries out his decree against me, and many such plans he still has in store." Job 23:14

f.

"In his heart a man plans his course, but the Lord determines his steps." Proverbs 16:9

g.

"A man's steps are directed by the Lord. How then can anyone understand his own way?" Proverbs 20:24

h.

"I know, O Lord, that a man's life is not his own; it is not for man to direct his steps." Jeremiah 10:23

i.

" 'For I know the plans I have for you,' declares the Lord, 'plans to prosper you and not to harm you, plans to give you hope and a future.' " Jeremiah 29:11

j.

"This man was handed over to you by God's set purpose and foreknowledge; and you, with the help of wicked men, put him to death by nailing him to the cross." Acts 2:23

k.

"It is not whether a hand grabs your hand and rescues you from the carnage; it is that no matter what happens, his strength empowers you to rise beyond the devastation."

Ravi Zacharias

"They did what your power and will had decided beforehand should happen." Acts 4:28

l.

"From one man he made every nation of men, that they should inhabit the whole earth; and he determined the times set for them and the exact places where they should live." Acts 17:26

m.

"And we know that in all things God works for the good of those who love him, who have been called according to his purpose." Romans 8:28

n.

"Being confident of this, that he who began a good work in you will carry it on to completion until the day of Christ Jesus." Philippians 1:6

o.

48. After examining these Scriptures, how are you more confident that God has a plan and purpose for your life?

IX. GOD SUSTAINS

The Hebrew word for "sustain" as it is used in the Old Testament generally means to prop up, to lean against, to bear up, to hold, or to stand fast. Have you ever felt as if you needed to be propped up?

"I lie down and sleep; I wake again, because the Lord sustains me." Psalm 3:5

"Cast your cares on the Lord and he will sustain you; he will never let the righteous fall." Psalm 55:22

"A man's spirit sustains him in sickness, but a crushed spirit who can bear?" Proverbs 18:14

49. Can you point to a time in your life when you knew that God was propping or holding you up?

50. Do you see a correlation between your faith and your strength?

SUMMARY

We think of the word "cope" as a way to deal with or overcome difficulties in our lives. The original meaning of cope, however, was a long cape or cloak, especially for outdoor wear. It also referred to a hooded ecclesiastical vestment, a covering. Have you ever thought of coping as a covering, something to protect you from the outside elements? That is exactly what God does for us—He covers us and protects us. Because we are assured that He hears us, He knows us, He is good, He loves us, He is with us, He is in us, He has plans for us, and He sustains us, we thus can find strength to go on . . . to do the next right thing.

"He will cover you with his feathers, and under
his wings you will find refuge;
his faithfulness will be your shield and rampart."
Psalm 91:4

CHAPTER 8

STRENGTHENING

"My soul is weary with sorrow; strengthen me according to your word."
Psalm 119:28

INTRODUCTION

Coping can bring comfort and strength. Did you know that the word comfort literally means "to make strong"? Where can you find comfort? How can you become strong?

Sometimes in looking for strength, we look to others, to things, even to ourselves. At times, I have found strength in all of these. At times, I have found strength in none of them. One way to gain physical strength is to lift weights. Lifting weights is hard but beneficial. Did you know that with training you can lift more than your body weight? There is a spiritual parallel here. I know of only one true source of strength and comfort. You will only find it in yourself *if God resides in you . . . "with the strength God provides, so that in all things God may be praised through Jesus Christ"* (1 Peter 4:11b).

THINKING IT OVER

1. What gives you comfort during difficult times?

2. What gives you strength when you are feeling vulnerable?

THINKING IN DEPTH

Bad things happen.

- Things break.
- People die.
- Planes crash.
- Babies die.
- Cars collide.
- Flowers die.
- Bones break.
- Muscles ache.
- Feelings get hurt.
- People say mean things.
- People get bored.
- Green lights turn red.
- Dust falls.
- People get tired.
- Mistakes happen.
- Gravity pulls things down.
- Food spoils.
- People get sick.
- Tires go flat.
- Bank accounts run out of cash.
- Cars run out of gas.

> "Bad days don't perhaps mean bad things have happened to me, but that I have handled whatever has happened particularly badly."
>
> **Denise Sproul**

This isn't meant to depress you, just to remind you that bad things do happen. Granted, there are degrees of "bad," just as there are degrees of "good." One person may think she is having a bad day because she missed the city bus, at the very same time another women learns her child has been killed by a school bus. That things do go wrong should not surprise us. It should not defeat us either. The inevitability of bad things happening should prepare us to be on guard. We should plan for this eventuality. We should come to terms with it. In this chapter, we will look at how God can bring good out of bad. Just as we focused in the last chapter on God's truths as they relate to coping, we will now look at two major principles that will further help us cope with the bad things in our lives: God's Sovereignty and God's Mysterious Ways. Through these principles we will discover the gold to be mined from trials and suffering, and ways to find comfort and strength.

The Inevitability of Trouble

> *"The Lord is a refuge for the oppressed, a stronghold in times of trouble."* Psalm 9:9

> *"Even though I walk through the valley of the shadow of death, I will fear no evil, for you are with me; your rod and your staff, they comfort me."* Psalm 23:4

> *"The troubles of my heart have multiplied; free me from my anguish."* Psalm 25:17

"Though an army besiege me, my heart will not fear; though war break out against me, even then will I be confident." Psalm 27:3

"For in the day of trouble he will keep me safe in his dwelling; he will hide me in the shelter of his tabernacle and set me high upon a rock." Psalm 27:5

"God is our refuge and strength, an ever-present help in trouble." Psalm 46:1

"For my soul is full of trouble and my life draws near the grave." Psalm 88:3

"Trouble and distress have come upon me, but your commands are my delight." Psalm 119:143

"Though I walk in the midst of trouble, you preserve my life; you stretch out your hand against the anger of my foes, with your right hand you save me." Psalm 138:7

"Say to those with fearful hearts, 'Be strong, do not fear; your God will come, he will come with vengeance; with divine retribution he will come to save you.' " Isaiah 35:4

"I have no peace, no quietness; I have no rest, but only turmoil." Job 3:26

"You will hear of wars and rumors of wars, but see to it that you are not alarmed. Such things must happen, but the end is still to come." Matthew 24:6

". . . who comforts us in all our troubles, so that we can comfort those in any trouble with the comfort we ourselves have received from God." 2 Corinthians 1:4

"We are hard pressed on every side, but not crushed; perplexed, but not in despair . . ." 2 Corinthians 4:8

"For when we came into Macedonia, this body of ours had no rest, but we were harassed at every turn—conflicts on the outside, fears within." 2 Corinthians 7:5

"Evidently some people are throwing you into confusion and are trying to pervert the gospel of Christ." Galatians 1:7b

"Finally, let no one cause me trouble, for I bear on my body the marks of Jesus." Galatians 6:17

"I have taken great pains [in my trouble KJV*] to provide for the temple of the Lord a hundred thousand talents of gold, a million talents of silver, quantities of bronze and iron too great to be weighed, and wood and stone. And you may add to them."* 1 Chronicles 22:14

1. Looking at the Scriptures above, what are some of the words and phrases used to describe trouble?

2. Was Job exempt from trouble because he was godly?

3. What does 2 Corinthians 1:4 tell us can be a good result of trouble in our lives?

4. According to Psalm 46:1, where does our help come from?

> "Sovereignty is not God's plan for evil, but His boundaries around it."
>
> **Charles Price**

God Is Sovereign

When we say that God is sovereign, we mean that He has supreme power. The word sovereign means "of the most exalted kind," "of an unqualified nature," "unlimited in extent." Others have explained sovereignty this way:

- "His hand may be hidden but his rule is absolute."[1] J. I. Packer

- "The root misunderstanding for pagans in all ages concerns the sovereignty of God."[2] Michael Horton

In the following Scriptures, we will look at some of the characteristics of God's sovereignty.

> "I am the Lord, and there is no other; apart from me there is no God. I will strengthen you, though you have not acknowledged me, so that from the rising of the sun to the place of its setting men may know there is none besides me. I am the Lord, and there is no other. I form the light and create darkness, I bring prosperity and create disaster; I, the Lord, do all these things." Isaiah 45:5-7

> "The Lord has established his throne in heaven, and his kingdom rules over all." Psalm 103:19

> "Our God is in heaven; he does whatever pleases him." Psalm 115:3

> "You discern my going out and my lying down; you are familiar with all my ways. Before a word is on my tongue you know it completely, O Lord." Psalm 139:3-4

> "Your eyes saw my unformed body. All the days ordained for me were written in your book before one of them came to be." Psalm 139:16

"'The decision is announced by messengers, the holy ones declare the verdict, so that the living may know that the Most High is sovereign over the kingdoms of men and gives them to anyone he wishes and sets over them the lowliest of men.' " Daniel 4:17

"You will be driven away from people and will live with the wild animals; you will eat grass like cattle and be drenched with the dew of heaven. Seven times will pass by for you until you acknowledge that the Most High is sovereign over the kingdoms of men and gives them to anyone he wishes." Daniel 4:25

"All the peoples of the earth are regarded as nothing. He does as he pleases with the powers of heaven and the peoples of the earth. No one can hold back his hand or say to him: 'What have you done?' " Daniel 4:35

"Now I, Nebuchadnezzar, praise and exalt and glorify the King of heaven, because everything he does is right and all his ways are just." Daniel 4:37a

"[11] Yet, before the twins were born or had done anything good or bad—in order that God's purpose in election might stand . . .[14] What then shall we say? Is God unjust? Not at all! [15] For he says to Moses, 'I will have mercy on whom I have mercy, and I will have compassion on whom I have compassion.' " Romans 9:11-15 [See also Exodus 33:19.]

" 'Who has ever given to God, that God should repay him?' For from him and through him and to him are all things. To him be the glory forever! Amen." Romans 11:35-36 [See also Job 41:11.]

"Ah, Sovereign Lord, you have made the heavens and the earth by your great power and outstretched arm. Nothing is too hard for you." Jeremiah 32:17

"I am the Lord, the God of all mankind. Is anything too hard for me?" Jeremiah 32:27

"For nothing is impossible with God." Luke 1:37

"Jesus replied, 'What is impossible with men is possible with God.' " Luke 18:27

"In him we were also chosen, having been predestined according to the plan of him who works out everything in conformity with the purpose of his will . . ." Ephesians 1:11

"The God who made the world and everything in it is the Lord of heaven and earth and does not live in temples built by hands. And he is not served by human hands, as if he needed anything, because he himself gives all men life and breath and everything else." Acts 17:24-25

5. Having read the Scriptures above, how would you define God's sovereignty?

6. Psalm 115:3 and Daniel 4:35 tell us that God does whatever pleases Him. How do we know that God will not use His power unrighteously? See Daniel 4:37 and Romans 9:14.

How Does God's Sovereignty Strengthen Us?

How does knowing about God's sovereignty strengthen us? The Heidelberg Catechism asks a similar question: (Question 28) "What advantage is it to us to know that God has created, and by his providence does still uphold all things?"[3] The catechism's answer is: "We can be patient when things go against us, thankful when things go well, and for the future we can have good confidence in our faithful God and Father that nothing will separate us from his love . . . "[4]

Distrusting God's sovereignty and providence is to think we know what is best—that what God has given us is not good enough.

By trusting God's sovereignty, we learn that:

(1) God allows trouble (Matthew 24:6).

(2) Good can come from bad (2 Corinthians 1:4).

(3) God can work through bad to produce good (Genesis 50:20).

> *"Peace I leave with you; my peace I give you. I do not give to you as the world gives. Do not let your hearts be troubled and do not be afraid."* John 14:27

(4) Therefore: Don't let this trouble:

   a. rob you of His peace or

   b. rule your hearts

> *"When he heard this, Jesus said, 'This sickness will not end in death. No, it is for God's glory so that God's Son may be glorified through it.'"* John 11:4 [speaking of Lazarus]

> *"'Neither this man nor his parents sinned,' said Jesus, 'but this happened so that the work of God might be displayed in his life.'"* John 9:2 [speaking of the man born blind]

7. According to these Scriptures, there was a reason for the trouble in these men's lives. What was that reason?

    a. John 11:4

    b. John 9:2

Larry Crabb said, "Live long enough and important dreams will shatter. Things will go wrong that God will not fix."[5] Thomas Watson said, "Poison is medicinable."[6] God never said "bad things" won't happen. He said He would make it right. Romans 8:28 says, *"And we know that in all things God works for the good of those who love him, who have been called according to his purpose."* Those who love Him, trust Him. They take what is handed to them and work through the pain so that they glorify Christ and fulfill His purpose for them. The bad things would not work for good—unless we worked for His good, by His grace.

> *"The Lord Almighty has sworn, 'Surely, as I have planned, so it will be, and as I have purposed, so it will stand' . . . For the Lord Almighty has purposed, and who can thwart him? His hand is stretched out, and who can turn it back?"* Isaiah 14:24, 27

8. What does Isaiah 14:24, 27 tell us about God's will?

9. Elisabeth Elliot said, "Frequently my will must be undone for God's will to be done."[7] What does this statement mean to you now?

There is good and bad on this earth. The problem of evil sabotaging good is as ancient as the Garden of Eden. It is the question debated in Job, one of the oldest books of the Bible. Job wrestled with the terrible troubles in his life, just as we wrestle with the troubles in our lives. But he never questioned God's sovereignty. And he learned that the will of God has to do more with character than circumstances. What's important is how we handle, react, and work through these situations. Do you think that you would be able to stand with Job in saying, *"Though he slay me, yet will I hope in him"* (13:15)?

God's Ways Are Incomprehensible

It does no good to try to "figure out" God. He cannot be comprehended. He is beyond our capacity to understand in totality. Some of the world's most respected theologians have said the following about the incomprehensibility of God.

- "For were the works of God readily understandable by human reason, they would be neither wonderful nor unspeakable."[8] Thomas à Kempis

- "The incomprehensibility of God does not mean that we know nothing about God. Rather it means that our knowledge is partial and limited . . . there is always more to God than we apprehend."[9] R. C. Sproul

> "Take heed of imagining that God's thoughts are as thy thoughts, and his ways as thy ways."
>
> **Charles H. Spurgeon**

" 'For my thoughts are not your thoughts, neither are your ways my ways,' declares the Lord. 'As the heavens are higher than the earth, so are my ways higher than your ways and my thoughts than your thoughts.' " Isaiah 55:8-9

"Do you not know? Have you not heard? The Lord is the everlasting God, the Creator of the ends of the earth. He will not grow tired or weary, and his understanding no one can fathom." Isaiah 40:28

"But who are you, O man, to talk back to God? 'Shall what is formed say to him who formed it,' "Why did you make me like this?" ' " Romans 9:20

"Oh, the depth of the riches of the wisdom and knowledge of God! How unsearchable his judgments, and his paths beyond tracing out! 'Who has known the mind of the Lord? Or who has been his counselor?' 'Who has ever given to God, that God should repay him?' For from him and through him and to him are all things. To him be the glory forever! Amen." Romans 11:33-36 [See also Isaiah 40:13.]

"Can you fathom the mysteries of God? Can you probe the limits of the Almighty? They are higher than the heavens—what can you do? They are deeper than the depths of the grave—what can you know? Their measure is longer than the earth and wider than the sea." Job 11:7-9

"Such knowledge is too wonderful for me, too lofty for me to attain." Psalm 139:6

"Call to me and I will answer you and tell you great and unsearchable things you do not know." Jeremiah 33:3

10. What phrase in Jeremiah 33:3 tells you that you can rely on God?

11. Does it comfort you to know that no one has ever known the mind of God or been His counselor? Why?

12. Read Job 38. Why do you think God chose to answer Job in this way?

God's Ways Are Mysterious

Billy Graham often speaks of "the mystery and reality of evil and suffering." Mystery implies that we do not understand or cannot comprehend something. God can be inferred from what we see through a microscope and telescope. But neither one of these devices can contain or define Him. The smartest people in the world recognize their ineptness at understanding God. The vast libraries of the world do not even begin to understand Him. It's simple: He's infinite, we're not.

You've probably heard that "men are from Mars and women from Venus." But God is from heaven and we're here on earth. He was here even before the beginning of time. We're only here now. It is hard enough to comprehend what has happened to us, much less to comprehend God.

> *"I do not want you to be ignorant of this mystery, brothers, so that you may not be conceited. . ."* Romans 11:25

> *"Now to him who is able to establish you by my gospel and the proclamation of Jesus Christ, according to the revelation of the mystery hidden for long ages past . . ."* Romans 16:25

> *"Surely you have heard about the administration of God's grace that was given to me for you, that is, the mystery made known to me by revelation, as I have already written briefly. In reading this, then, you will be able to understand my insight into the mystery of Christ, which was not made known to men in other generations as it has now been revealed by the Spirit to God's holy apostles and prophets. This mystery is that through the gospel the Gentiles are heirs together with Israel, members together of one body, and sharers together in the promise in Christ Jesus. I became a servant of this gospel by the gift of God's grace given me through the working of his power. Although I am less than the least of all God's people, this grace was given me: to preach to the Gentiles the unsearchable riches of Christ, and to make plain to everyone the administration of this mystery, which for ages past was kept hidden in God, who created all things."* Ephesians 3:2-9

> *"Pray also for me, that whenever I open my mouth, words may be given me so that I will fearlessly make known the mystery of the gospel . . ."* Ephesians 6:19

> *"I have become its servant by the commission God gave me to present to you the word of God in its fullness—the mystery that has been kept hidden for ages and generations, but is now disclosed to the saints."* Colossians 1:25, 26

> *"And pray for us, too, that God may open a door for our message, so that we may proclaim the mystery of Christ, for which I am in chains."* Colossians 4:3

> *"Listen, I tell you a mystery: We will not all sleep, but we will all be changed . . ."* 1 Corinthians 15:51

"Mystery is not the absence of meaning, but the presence of more meaning than we can comprehend."

Philip Yancey

"No, we speak of God's secret wisdom, a wisdom that has been hidden and that God destined for our glory before time began. None of the rulers of this age understood it, for if they had, they would not have crucified the Lord of glory. However, as it is written: 'no eye has seen, no ear has heard, no mind has conceived what God has prepared for those who love him'—but God has revealed it to us by his Spirit. The Spirit searches all things, even the deep things of God. For who among men knows the thoughts of a man except the man's spirit within him? In the same way no one knows the thoughts of God except the Spirit of God. We have not received the spirit of the world but the Spirit who is from God, that we may understand what God has freely given us. This is what we speak, not in words taught us by human wisdom but in words taught by the Spirit, expressing spiritual truths in spiritual words. The man without the Spirit does not accept the things that come from the Spirit of God, for they are foolishness to him, and he cannot understand them, because they are spiritually discerned. The spiritual man makes judgments about all things, but he himself is not subject to any man's judgment: 'For who has known the mind of the Lord that he may instruct him?' But we have the mind of Christ." 1 Corinthians 2:7-16 [See also Isaiah 64:4 and 40:15.]

13. How does God reveal mysteries to us?

14. Does God leave mystery in our lives? Why?

How Does God Comfort Us?

Second Corinthians 1:1-11 offers a beautiful tribute to the God of all comfort. In explaining to the Corinthians what he had suffered in the province of Asia, Paul says: *"But this happened that we might not rely on ourselves but on God, who raises the dead"* (v. 9). A God who is sovereign, whose ways are incomprehensible, who is not only vaster than the universe but is the Creator of the universe—that God is big enough to carry our burdens and help us through our deepest valleys. Don't look for your comfort in things, other people, rationale, or even philosophy. Look to the Comforter himself, the source of comfort, for He is true comfort. When Jesus told His disciples that He was leaving, that He was going to die, He said: *"I will ask the Father, and He will give you another Counselor to be with you forever"* (John 14:16). The Greek word for "counselor" used here is "paraklētos." "Para" means *by the side* and "kaleō" means *to call*. This is a call hither to speak, especially cheerfully, to encourage, to help. The word is also translated into Helper, Advocate, and Comforter. Note other references:

"Then the church throughout Judea, Galilee and Samaria enjoyed a time of peace. It was strengthened; and encouraged by the Holy Spirit, it grew in numbers, living in the fear of the Lord." Acts 9:31

*"And I will ask the Father, and he will give you another Counselor to be with you forever . . ."*John 14:16

*"But the Counselor, the Holy Spirit, whom the Father will send in my name, will teach you all things and will remind you of everything I have said to you."*John 14:26

*"When the Counselor comes, whom I will send to you from the Father, the Spirit of truth who goes out from the Father, he will testify about me . . ."*John 15:26

*"But I tell you the truth: It is for your good that I am going away. Unless I go away, the Counselor will not come to you; but if I go, I will send him to you."*John 16:7

*"[9] However, as it is written: 'no eye has seen, no ear has heard, no mind has conceived what God has prepared for those who love him'—[10] but God has revealed it to us by his Spirit. The Spirit searches all things, even the deep things of God . . . [11b] no one knows the thoughts of God except the Spirit of God. [12] We have not received the spirit of the world but the Spirit who is from God, that we may understand what God has freely given us."*1 Corinthians 2:9-10, 11b-12

*"[3] Not only so, but we also rejoice in our sufferings, because we know that suffering produces perseverance; [4] perseverance, character; and character, hope. [5] And hope does not disappoint us, because God has poured out his love into our hearts by the Holy Spirit, whom he has given us."*Romans 5:3-5

*"When you pass through the waters, I will be with you; and when you pass through the rivers, they will not sweep over you. When you walk through the fire, you will not be burned; the flames will not set you ablaze."*Isaiah 43:2

*"Shout for joy, O heavens; rejoice, O earth; burst into song, O mountains! For the Lord comforts his people and will have compassion on his afflicted ones."*Isaiah 49:13

*" 'So then, don't be afraid. I will provide for you and your children.' And he reassured them and spoke kindly to them."*Genesis 50:21

*"Have I not commanded you? Be strong and courageous. Do not be terrified; do not be discouraged, for the Lord your God will be with you wherever you go."*Joshua 1:9

*"And surely I am with you always, to the very end of the age."*Matthew 28:20b

15. In the introduction to this chapter, we said that the original meaning of the word comfort is "to make strong." According to Romans 5:3-4, what does suffering work in us?

16. As we have seen, the Holy Spirit has many names. According to the following verses, what does He do for (in) us?

    a. John 14:16

    b. John 14:26

    c. John 15:26

17. According to the 1 Corinthians 2 passage, how does the Holy Spirit help us *"understand what God has freely given us?"*

How Can We Mine Gold from the Pits?

Romans 5:3-4 tells us to "rejoice in our sufferings" because in the process of undergoing trials and suffering—with the help of the Holy Spirit—we learn perseverance, which builds character, which gives us hope. Read what others have had to say about the nature and effects of trials.

- "Afflictions are purifying."[10] Thomas Watson

- "Afflictions teach us to pray better."[11] Watson

- "The meaning of trial is not only to test worthiness, but to increase it."[12] Mrs. Charles Cowman

- ". . . difficulties, trials, and emergencies . . . these are divinely provided vessels for the Holy Spirit to fill . . . opportunities for receiving new blessings and deliverances . . . Bring these vessels to God. Hold them steadily before Him in faith and prayer."[13] Cowman

- "Difficulty is not to be feared or denied, it is to be used."[14] Blaise Pascal

- "Healing will begin only when we're willing to accept that life is difficult."[15] Pascal

- "Remember the good in the days of thine affliction, and remember thine affliction in the days of rejoicing."[16] Pascal

- "Whenever we place a higher priority on solving our problems than on pursuing God, we are immoral."[17] Larry Crabb

"We must remember that a trial is a trial for one reason only; we do not like it!"

Thomas Boston

• "Satan . . . who seeks through affliction to turn believers away from the gospel (1 Thessalonians 3:5) to hinder God's servants in their ministry (1 Thessalonians 2:18) . . . Satan's main objective is to frustrate."[18] George E. Ladd

18. According to these quotations, what positive things can come about as the result of trials?

19. From George Ladd's quote, what does Satan hope to accomplish through our trials?

20. Write what you learn about trials, as you examine the following Scriptures:

"In this you greatly rejoice, though now for a little while you may have had to suffer grief in all kinds of trials. These have come so that your faith—of greater worth than gold, which perishes even though refined by fire—may be proved genuine and may result in praise, glory and honor when Jesus Christ is revealed. Though you have not seen him, you love him; and even though you do not see him now, you believe in him and are filled with an inexpressible and glorious joy . . ." 1 Peter 1:6-8

a.

"But how is it to your credit if you receive a beating for doing wrong and endure it? But if you suffer for doing good and you endure it, this is commendable before God. To this you were called, because Christ suffered for you, leaving you an example, that you should follow in his steps." 1 Peter 2:20-21

b.

"I tell you the truth, you will weep and mourn while the world rejoices. You will grieve, but your grief will turn to joy." John 16:20

c.

"He replied, 'You are talking like a foolish woman. Shall we accept good from God, and not trouble?' In all this, Job did not sin in what he said." Job 2:10

d.

"When you are in distress and all these things have happened to you, then in later days you will return to the Lord your God and obey him." Deuteronomy 4:30

"The success that God gives us may not be to get out of the circumstances but to have the grace in order to endure the circumstances."

Thomas Boston

e.

"Remember how the Lord your God led you all the way in the desert these forty years, to humble you and to test you in order to know what was in your heart, whether or not you would keep his commands . . . He gave you manna to eat in the desert, something your fathers had never known, to humble and to test you so that in the end it might go well with you." Deuteronomy 8:2, 16

f.

"Consider it pure joy, my brothers, whenever you face trials of many kinds . . . Perseverance must finish its work so that you may be mature and complete, not lacking anything." James 1:2, 4

g.

"[28] And we know that in all things God works for the good of those who love him, who have been called according to his purpose . . . [35-39] Who shall separate us from the love of Christ? Shall trouble or hardship or persecution or famine or nakedness or danger or sword? As it is written: 'For your sake we face death all day long; we are considered as sheep to be slaughtered.' No, in all these things we are more than conquerors through him who loved us. For I am convinced that neither death nor life, neither angels nor demons, neither the present nor the future, nor any powers, neither height nor depth, nor anything else in all creation, will be able to separate us from the love of God that is in Christ Jesus our Lord." Romans 8:28, 35-39

h.

"I served the Lord with great humility and with tears, although I was severely tested . . ." Acts 20:19

i.

"So this is what the Sovereign Lord says: 'See, I lay a stone in Zion, a tested stone, a precious cornerstone for a sure foundation; the one who trusts will never be dismayed.'" Isaiah 28:16

j.

"We must go through many hardships to enter the kingdom of God." Acts 14:22b

k.

"And hope does not disappoint us, because God has poured out his love into our hearts by the Holy Spirit, whom he has given us." Romans 5:5

l.

"Dear friends, do not be surprised at the painful trial you are suffering, as though some thing strange were happening to you." 1 Peter 4:12

m.

"But rejoice that you participate in the sufferings of Christ, so that you may be overjoyed when his glory is revealed." 1 Peter 4:13

n.

"For our light and momentary troubles are achieving for us an eternal glory that far outweighs them all. So we fix our eyes not on what is seen, but on what is unseen. For what is seen is temporary, but what is unseen is eternal." 2 Corinthians 4:17-18

o.

"When my heart was grieved and my spirit embittered, I was senseless and ignorant; I was a brute beast before you. Yet I am always with you; you hold me by my right hand. You guide me with your counsel, and afterward you will take me into glory. Whom have I in heaven but you? And earth has nothing I desire besides you." Psalm 73:21-25

p.

What Can We Learn from the Schoolhouse of Suffering?

There are degrees of pain. We may undergo a trial and not actually suffer. Suffering brings the pain home in a sustained and intimate way. When Paul was ridiculed and run out of town time after time, we can be sure he felt humiliation, sorrow, even confusion. However, when he was beaten and put in chains, he learned the difference between trials and suffering. Read what others have had to say about suffering.

> "Suffering, the chisel to shape the soul."
>
> **Howard G. Hendricks**

- "He who suffers most has most to give."[19] Mrs. Charles Cowman

- "Suffering . . . it will always reveal the core of who we are. Affliction doesn't teach us about ourselves from a textbook, it uses the stuff inside us."[20] Joni E. Tada

- "There is nothing we can do with suffering except to suffer it."[21] C. S. Lewis

- "Suffering, in fact, is guaranteed for anyone who takes on the task of living."[22] Tim Hansel

- "Suffering is either having what you don't want or not having what you want."[23] Elisabeth Elliot

- "There are only two things that pierce the human heart: beauty and affliction."[24] Simone Weil

21. Having read these quotations, what do you think of suffering?

Read the following Scriptures about suffering. Beware: God uses pain to pull back the covers, to turn up the heat . . . to discover what is in us and what is missing.

22. After each Scripture, list anything you can learn about suffering.

> *"You intended to harm me, but God intended it for good to accomplish what is now being done, the saving of many lives."* Genesis 50:20

a.

> *"Endure hardship as discipline; God is treating you as sons. For what son is not disciplined by his father? If you are not disciplined (and everyone undergoes discipline), then you are illegitimate children and not true sons. Moreover, we have all had human fathers who disciplined us and we respected them for it. How much more should we submit to the Father of our spirits and live! Our fathers disciplined us for a little while as they thought best; but God disciplines us for our good, that we may share in his holiness. No discipline seems pleasant at the time, but painful. Later on, however, it produces a harvest of righteousness and peace for those who have been trained by it."* Hebrews 12:7-11

b.

"In bringing many sons to glory, it was fitting that God, for whom and through whom everything exists, should make the author of their salvation perfect through suffering." Hebrews 2:10

c.

"Although he was a son, he learned obedience from what he suffered and, once made perfect, he became the source of eternal salvation for all who obey him . . ." Hebrews 5:8-9

d.

"Remember those earlier days after you had received the light, when you stood your ground in a great contest in the face of suffering. Sometimes you were publicly exposed to insult and persecution; at other times you stood side by side with those who were so treated. You sympathized with those in prison and joyfully accepted the confiscation of your property, because you knew that you yourselves had better and lasting possessions. So do not throw away your confidence; it will be richly rewarded. You need to persevere so that when you have done the will of God, you will receive what he has promised." Hebrews 10:32-36

e.

"Blessed are those who are persecuted because of righteousness, for theirs is the kingdom of heaven. Blessed are you when people insult you, persecute you and falsely say all kinds of evil against you because of me. Rejoice and be glad, because great is your reward in heaven, for in the same way they persecuted the prophets who were before you." Matthew 5:10-12

f.

"If the world hates you, keep in mind that it hated me first. If you belonged to the world, it would love you as its own. As it is, you do not belong to the world, but I have chosen you out of the world. That is why the world hates you. Remember the words I spoke to you: 'No servant is greater than his master.' If they persecuted me, they will persecute you also. If they obeyed my teaching, they will obey yours also. They will treat you this way because of my name, for they do not know the One who sent me. If I had not come and spoken to them, they would not be guilty of sin. Now, however, they have no excuse for their sin. He who hates me hates my Father as well." John 15:18-23

"Jesus did not come to explain away suffering; he came to fill it with his presence."

Paul Claudel

g.

"Peace I leave with you; my peace I give you. I do not give to you as the world gives. Do not let your hearts be troubled and do not be afraid." John 14:27

h.

"Not only so, but we also rejoice in our sufferings, because we know that suffering produces perseverance; perseverance, character; and character, hope. And hope does not disappoint us, because God has poured out his love into our hearts by the Holy Spirit, whom he has given us." Romans 5:3-5

i.

"Now if we are children, then we are heirs—heirs of God and co-heirs with Christ, if indeed we share in his sufferings in order that we may also share in his glory. I consider that our present sufferings are not worth comparing with the glory that will be revealed in us." Romans 8:17-18

j.

"Those whom I love I rebuke and discipline. So be earnest and repent."
Revelation 3:19

k.

"In fact, everyone who wants to live a godly life in Christ Jesus will be persecuted . . ."
2 Timothy 3:12

l.

"No temptation has seized you except what is common to man. And God is faithful; he will not let you be tempted beyond what you can bear. But when you are tempted, he will also provide a way out so that you can stand up under it."
1 Corinthians 10:13

m.

"If one part suffers, every part suffers with it; if one part is honored, every part rejoices with it." 1 Corinthians 12:26

n.

"Praise be to the God and Father of our Lord Jesus Christ, the Father of compassion and the God of all comfort, who comforts us in all our troubles, so that we can comfort those in any trouble with the comfort we ourselves have received from God. For just as the sufferings of Christ flow over into our lives, so also through Christ our comfort overflows." 2 Corinthians 1:3-5

o.

"But we have this treasure in jars of clay to show that this all-surpassing power is from God and not from us. We are hard pressed on every side, but not crushed; perplexed, but not in despair; persecuted, but not abandoned; struck down, but not destroyed. We always carry around in our body the death of Jesus, so that the life of Jesus may also be revealed in our body." 2 Corinthians 4:7-10

p.

"But he said to me, 'My grace is sufficient for you, for my power is made perfect in weakness.' Therefore I will boast all the more gladly about my weaknesses, so that Christ's power may rest on me." 2 Corinthians 12:9

q.

"For it has been granted to you on behalf of Christ not only to believe on him, but also to suffer for him . . ." Philippians 1:29

r.

"Do not be anxious about anything, but in everything, by prayer and petition, with thanksgiving, present your requests to God. And the peace of God, which transcends all understanding, will guard your hearts and your minds in Christ Jesus." Philippians 4:6-7

s.

"But even if you should suffer for what is right, you are blessed. 'Do not fear what they fear; do not be frightened' . . . It is better, if it is God's will, to suffer for doing good than for doing evil." 1 Peter 3:14, 17 [See also Isaiah 8:12.]

t.

"Therefore, since Christ suffered in his body, arm yourselves also with the same attitude, because he who has suffered in his body is done with sin . . . However, if you suffer as a Christian, do not be ashamed, but praise God that you bear that name . . . So then, those who suffer according to God's will should commit themselves to their faithful Creator and continue to do good." 1 Peter 4:1, 16, 19

u.

"And the God of all grace, who called you to his eternal glory in Christ, after you have suffered a little while, will himself restore you and make you strong, firm and steadfast." 1 Peter 5:10

v.

". . . because you know that the testing of your faith develops perseverance. Perseverance must finish its work so that you may be mature and complete, not lacking anything." James 1:3, 4

w.

23. Read the first chapter of 1 Peter. How would you summarize the main points, as they relate to suffering?

24. Whom does your suffering serve? God or the devil?

Hebrews 10:34 mentions that the Hebrew Christians had *"sympathized with those in prison."* The original Greek word for sympathize means to "suffer with another." *Webster's Dictionary* also points to the origin of sympathy as "syn pathos," to share in suffering or grief. The Greek word for pathos derives from the word for suffering. As we suffer, it is important to realize that just *enduring* it is not the point. God expects us to use our suffering to benefit others, *"so that we can comfort those in any trouble with the comfort we ourselves have received from God"* (2 Corinthians 1:4b).

Comforting Widows

How does God feel about widows? Are they important to Him? Let's look at what Scripture says about widows.

"In those days when the number of disciples was increasing, the Grecian Jews among them complained against the Hebraic Jews because their widows were being overlooked in the daily distribution of food." Acts 6:1 [They were not to be overlooked.]

"Religion that God our Father accepts as pure and faultless is this: to look after orphans and widows in their distress and to keep oneself from being polluted by the world." James 1:27 [God wants them to be looked after.]

"Give proper recognition to those widows who are really in need." 1 Timothy 5:3 [They were to be given proper recognition.]

"The Lord tears down the proud man's house but he keeps the widow's boundaries intact." Proverbs 15:25 [The Lord loves them.]

"A father to the fatherless, a defender of widows, is God in his holy dwelling." Psalm 68:5 [God defends them.]

"He defends the cause of the fatherless and the widow, and loves the alien, giving food and clothing." Deuteronomy 10:18 [He defends and provides for them.]

"Seek justice, encourage the oppressed. Defend the cause of the fatherless, plead the case of the widow." Isaiah 1:17 [God exhorts His people to defend widows.]

"The Lord watches over the alien and sustains the fatherless and the widow, but he frustrates the ways of the wicked." Psalm 146:9 [The Lord watches over and sustains them.]

"Do not take advantage of a widow or an orphan." Exodus 22:22 [God doesn't want widows to be taken advantage of.]

Finding Strength

Widows are special to God. However, He knows how vulnerable they are, so He made it very clear that they were to be taken care of and not to be taken advantage of. As we all know, the world doesn't always listen to God's Word. Many widows have to struggle on their own to find their place in society. God knows that the vulnerable and lonely need comfort. Where do they turn when the world turns away? Where do they find true comfort and strength?

"He gives strength to the weary and increases the power of the weak." Isaiah 40:29

"So do not fear, for I am with you; do not be dismayed, for I am your God. I will strengthen you and help you; I will uphold you with my righteous right hand." Isaiah 41:10

"He makes my feet like the feet of a deer; he enables me to stand on the heights." Psalm 18:32

"The Lord is my light and my salvation—whom shall I fear? The Lord is the stronghold of my life—of whom shall I be afraid?" Psalm 27:1

"The Lord gives strength to his people; the Lord blesses his people with peace." Psalm 29:11

"God is our refuge and strength, an ever-present help in trouble." Psalm 46:1

"I will sing of your strength, in the morning I will sing of your love; for you are my fortress, my refuge in times of trouble." Psalm 59:16

"Your troops will be willing on your day of battle. Arrayed in holy majesty, from the womb of the dawn you will receive the dew of your youth." Psalm 110:3

"My soul is weary with sorrow; strengthen me according to your word." Psalm 119:28

[Jesus] *". . . sustaining all things by his powerful word."* Hebrews 1:3b

"The bolts of your gates will be iron and bronze, and your strength will equal your days." Deuteronomy 33:25

"No one will be able to stand up against you all the days of your life. As I was with Moses, so I will be with you; I will never leave you nor forsake you. Be strong and courageous, because you will lead these people to inherit the land I swore to their forefathers to give them. Be strong and very courageous. Be careful to obey all the law my servant Moses gave you; do not turn from it to the right or to the left, that you may be successful wherever you go. Do not let this Book of the Law depart from your mouth; meditate on it day and night, so that you may be careful to do everything written in it. Then you will be prosperous and successful. Have I not commanded you? Be strong and courageous. Do not be terrified; do not be discouraged, for the Lord your God will be with you wherever you go." Joshua 1:5-9

"With flattery he will corrupt those who have violated the covenant, but the people who know their God will firmly resist him." Daniel 11:32

"But he said to me, 'My grace is sufficient for you, for my power is made perfect in weakness.' Therefore I will boast all the more gladly about my weaknesses, so that Christ's power may rest on me. That is why, for Christ's sake, I delight in weaknesses, in insults, in hardships, in persecutions, in difficulties. For when I am weak, then I am strong." 2 Corinthians 12:9-10

"I pray that out of his glorious riches he may strengthen you with power through his Spirit in your inner being." Ephesians 3:16

25. According to Isaiah 40:29, to whom does God give strength?

26. How are the weary strengthened, according to Psalm 119:28?

27. According to Deuteronomy 33:25, what will our strength equal?

28. According to Daniel 11:32, what is the basis for the strength you need to resist the enemy?

29. What does Paul mean by saying, *"For when I am weak, then I am strong"* (2 Corinthians 9:10)? How has that been demonstrated in your life?

SUMMARY

When we think of comfort, we think of things like comfort food, comfortable clothes, comfortable surroundings, or people we are comfortable with. But we have seen that comfort through the lens of Scripture is not a warm and fuzzy concept. It is based on strength—which is what comfort means: "to make strong." In other words, to be comforted, to be made strong, we need Him.

Knowing that God is sovereign and incomprehensible reassures us that He is the source of true strength. Knowing that He cares for us on an intimate level, that He is personally involved in our daily lives, reassures us that He is the source of true comfort. The more faith we have in Him, the more strength we will have to cope with the trials and suffering in our lives. The more we seek to know Him, the more comfort we will receive. The more comfort we receive, the more we will be able to share with others.

"Wait for the Lord; be strong and take heart and wait for the Lord."
Psalm 27:14

CHAPTER 9

PRAYING

"Be still, and know that I am God . . ."
Psalm 46:10a

INTRODUCTION

To know God's will for our lives, God has given us two sources: the Bible and prayer. God speaks to us through both avenues. In the Bible we discover how God has worked in the past and what He will do in the future. We learn the broad principles of our faith and meet many men and women who modeled that faith, and many who didn't.

Prayer is approaching God in the present with our needs, our worship, our questions, our problems, our hunger, our love. It is the way we communicate with God and He with us. When you have lost a loved one, you long for the sound of his voice. You miss the conversations you had. It doesn't seem that anyone but God could fill the empty spaces with words as cherished as your loved one's. God can fill those spaces. And God will. He longs for your voice as much as you long for His.

THINKING IT OVER

1. How do you pray? Do you set aside a certain time every day for prayer?

2. Do your feel that your prayers aren't "good enough," that they are awkward and poorly articulated?

3. What would you like to change about your prayer life? How do you think you can make these changes?

THINKING IN DEPTH

Prayer is indispensable in strengthening us. It is probably the best "coping" method for those experiencing grief. But it is more than a method or "technique," as some contemporary counselors would have you believe. That is why we have devoted an entire chapter to prayer. Prayer is not just about getting. It is about giving. Read what others have said about prayer.

- "We focus on ourselves. But the prayers of the Bible have one characteristic in common: they always focus on the Person to whom the prayer is addressed."[1] Howard and William Hendricks

- "Always pray on the basis of the promises of God."[2] Hendricks and Hendricks

- "In your praying are you devoted to God, or your desire(s)?"[3] Oswald Chambers, paraphrase

- "When I pray do I try to see the bigger issues [redemption, sanctification] or do I only see my circumstances?"[4] Oswald Chambers

- "Prayer is not for the purpose of informing God . . . it is but to acknowledge He does know what we are in need of."[5] A. W. Pink

- "Prayer is a coming to God, telling Him my need, committing my way unto the Lord and leaving Him to deal with it as seemeth Him best."[6] A. W. Pink

- "Prayer is a two-way fellowship and communication with God . . . It is not a one-way conversation . . . Prayer includes listening . . . Prayer is a relationship, not just a religious activity."[7] Henry T. Blackaby

- "Prayer is nothing else but the soul's breathing itself into the bosom of its Father."[8] Thomas Watson

- "Prayer was never meant to be magic . . . it's an act of love."[9] Madeleine L'Engle

- "Prayer is a walkie-talkie for warfare, not a domestic intercom for increasing our conveniences. The point of prayer is empowering for mission."[10] John Piper

Now let's turn to what Scripture has to say about prayer.

"We have confidence before God and receive from him anything we ask, because we obey his commands and do what pleases him." 1 John 3:22

"This is the confidence we have in approaching God: that if we ask anything according to his will, he hears us. And if we know that he hears us—whatever we ask—we know that we have what we asked of him." 1 John 5:14-15

"Pray continually . . ." 1 Thessalonians 5:17

"As for me, far be it from me that I should sin against the Lord by failing to pray for you." 1 Samuel 12:23a

1. According to 1 John 3:22 and 5:14-15, what confidence should we have?

2. Is prayer incidental or intentional, according to 1 Thessalonians 5:17?

3. What does 1 Samuel 12:23 a call the failure to pray?

I. BENEFITS OF PRAYER

Read the following Scriptures to learn some of the benefits of prayer.

"Come near to God and he will come near to you." James 4:8a [to draw near to God]

"Jabez cried out to the God of Israel, 'Oh that you would bless me and enlarge my territory! Let your hand be with me, and keep me from harm so that I will be free from pain.'" 1 Chronicles 4:10 [for God to be with us]

"You will keep in perfect peace him whose mind is steadfast, because he trusts in you." Isaiah 26:3 [peace from keeping our minds on God]

"We demolish arguments and every pretension that sets itself up against the knowledge of God, and we take captive every thought to make it obedient to Christ." 2 Corinthians10:5 [to bring every thought to Him]

"And you have been given fullness in Christ, who is the head over every power and authority." Colossians 2:10 [for oneness with Him; see also John 17:11, 20-23]

"In the morning, O Lord, you hear my voice; in the morning I lay my requests before you and wait in expectation." Psalm 5:3 [for the Lord to hear us]

"Hear my voice according to Thy lovingkindness; Revive me, O Lord, according to Thine ordinances." Psalm 119:149 NASB [to be revived]

"Now, therefore, I pray thee, if I have found grace in thy sight, show me now thy way, that I may know thee, that I may find grace in thy sight . . ." Exodus 33:13 KJV [to show us His way; to find grace]

"For it is God who works in you to will and to act according to his good purpose." Philippians 2:13 [to work in us]

"And the peace of God, which transcends all understanding, will guard your hearts and your minds in Christ Jesus." Philippians 4:7 [to give us peace; to guard our hearts and minds; see also 1 Timothy 2:2]

II. REASONS FOR PRAYER

Examine the following Scriptures to understand some of the reasons we come to God in prayer.

". . . always giving thanks to God the Father for everything, in the name of our Lord Jesus Christ." Ephesians 5:20 [to give thanks]

"Then he prayed, 'O Lord, God of my master Abraham, give me success today, and show kindness to my master Abraham.' " Genesis 24:12 [for help]

"The people came to Moses and said, 'We sinned when we spoke against the Lord and against you. Pray that the Lord will take the snakes away from us.' So Moses prayed for the people." Numbers 21:7 [for relief]

"Ask the Lord of the harvest, therefore, to send out workers into his harvest field." Matthew 9:38 [for needs]

"If any of you lacks wisdom, he should ask God, who gives generously to all without finding fault, and it will be given to him." James 1:5 [for wisdom]

4. Can you think of some other reasons for prayer?

5. Are these reasons to pray important for you?

"Pray continually . . ." 1 Thessalonians 5:17

"God, whom I serve with my whole heart in preaching the gospel of his Son, is my witness how constantly I remember you in my prayers at all times . . ." Romans 1:9-10a

"Devote yourselves to prayer, being watchful and thankful." Colossians 4:2

"I want men everywhere to lift up holy hands in prayer . . ." 1 Timothy 2:8

". . . He is always wrestling in prayer for you, that you may stand firm in all the will of God, mature and fully assured." Colossians 4:12

6. According to 1 Thessalonians 5:17, Romans 1:9-10a, and Colossians 4:2, how often should we pray?

7. Where can we pray, according to 1 Timothy 2:8?

8. Is prayer always a fun and leisurely activity? What phrases from Colossians 4 reveal this?

III. OBSTACLES TO PRAYER

Sin is not the only thing that can block our prayers. Anxiety and frustration can too. Study the Scriptures below to see what interferes with your prayers.

9. Study the following Scriptures to see what obstacles or hindrances you can find and list them below.

"But your iniquities have separated you from your God; your sins have hidden his face from you, so that he will not hear." Isaiah 59:2

a.

"If I had cherished sin in my heart, the Lord would not have listened." Psalm 66:18

b.

"I want men everywhere to lift up holy hands in prayer, without anger or disputing." 1 Timothy 2:8

c.

"Do not be anxious about anything, but in everything, by prayer and petition, with thanksgiving, present your requests to God." Philippians 4:6

d.

"And when you stand praying, if you hold anything against anyone, forgive him, so that your Father in heaven may forgive you your sins." Mark 11:25

e.

"When he came back, he again found them sleeping, because their eyes were heavy. So he left them and went away once more and prayed the third time, saying the same thing." Matthew 26:43-44

f.

"And he spake a parable unto them to this end, that men ought always to pray, and not to faint." Luke 18:1 KJV

g.

"In the same way, the Spirit helps us in our weakness. We do not know what we ought to pray for, but the Spirit himself intercedes for us with groans that words cannot express." Romans 8:26

10. Now, according to Romans 8:26, who helps us in prayer?

"Father, if you are willing, take this cup from me; yet not my will, but yours be done." Luke 22:42

"And he who searches our hearts knows the mind of the Spirit, because the Spirit intercedes for the saints in accordance with God's will." Romans 8:27

"This is the confidence we have in approaching God: that if we ask anything according to his will, he hears us." 1 John 5:14

11. What qualification does God put on our prayers, according to Luke 22:42, Romans 8:27, and 1 John 5:14 above?

IV. TIMES FOR PRAYER

For much of recorded history, people have prayed at specific times of the day. We know that Daniel prayed three times a day (Daniel 6:10). The early disciples continued to follow Jewish prayer customs after the Resurrection. We read that Peter and John went up to the temple *"at the time of prayer—at three in the afternoon"* (Acts 3:1). Later Christians set even more times for prayer as worship became increasingly ritualized.

As you read the following Scriptures, think how often prayer should fill your days and nights.

IN THE MORNING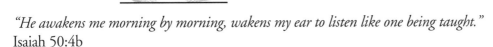

"He awakens me morning by morning, wakens my ear to listen like one being taught."
Isaiah 50:4b

"When I awake, I am still with you." Psalm 139:18b

"I awake again, because the Lord sustains me." Psalm 3:5

"Satisfy us in the morning with your unfailing love, that we may sing for joy and be glad all our days." Psalm 90:14

"But I will sing of your strength, in the morning I will sing of your love." Psalm 59:16

"In the morning, O Lord, you hear my voice; in the morning, I lay my requests before you and wait in expectation." Psalm 5:3

"It is good to praise the Lord . . . to proclaim your love in the morning . . ."
Psalm 92:1a, 2a

"Be our strength every morning . . ." Isaiah 33:2b

"Let the morning bring me word of your unfailing love, for I have put my trust in you. Show me the way I should go, for to you, I lift up my soul." Psalm 143:8

AT NIGHT

". . . when you are on your beds, search your hearts and be silent." Psalm 4:4

"I will lie down and sleep in peace, for you alone, O Lord, make me dwell in safety."
Psalm 4:8

"On my bed I remember you; I think of you through the watches of the night."
Psalm 63:6

". . . when you lie down, you will not be afraid; when you lie down, your sleep will be sweet." Proverbs 3:24

"Though you probe my heart and examine me at night . . ." Psalm 17:3

". . . at night his song is with me—a prayer to the God of my life." Psalm 42:8

"I will praise the Lord, who counsels me; even at night my heart instructs me. I have set the Lord always before me . . ." Psalm 16:7-8a

"It is good to praise the Lord . . . to proclaim . . . your faithfulness at night . . ." Psalm 92:1a-2b

"For He gives to His beloved even in his sleep." Psalm 127:2b NASB

"May my prayer be set before you like incense; may the lifting up of my hands be like the evening sacrifice." Psalm 141:2

"My Presence will go with you, and I will give you rest." Exodus 33:14

EVERY DAY

"Every day I will praise you and extol your name for ever and ever." Psalm 145:2

"Sing to the Lord, praise his name; proclaim his salvation day after day." Psalm 96:2

"Teach us to number our days aright, that we may gain a heart of wisdom." Psalm 90:12

"This is the day the Lord has made; let us rejoice and be glad in it." Psalm 118:24

"Now the Bereans . . . examined the Scriptures every day . . ." Acts 17:11

". . . inwardly we are being renewed day by day." 2 Corinthians 4:16

ALL DAY LONG

". . . and my hope is in you all day long." Psalm 25:5b

"My tongue will speak of your righteousness and of your praises all day long." Psalm 35:28

V. SAMPLES OF PRAYERS

A prayer doesn't have to be lofty and lengthy to be of value to God. The Bible is full of prayers—some beautifully lyrical, others simple and down to earth. It is not so much the packaging as the content that counts.

Jabez: *"Oh that you would bless me indeed, and enlarge my territory! Let your hand be with me, and keep me from harm so that I will be free from pain."* 1 Chronicles 4:10

Isaiah: *"Here am I. Send me!"* Isaiah 6:8b.

Hezekiah: *"Now, O Lord our God, deliver us . . . that all kingdoms on earth may know that you alone, O Lord, are God."* Isaiah 37:20

Stephen: *"Lord Jesus, receive my spirit . . . Lord, do not hold this sin against them."* Acts 7:59, 60.

Moses: *"If you are pleased with me, teach me your ways so I may know you and continue to find favor with you."* Exodus 33:13

Samson: *"O Sovereign Lord, remember me. O God, please strengthen me . . ."* Judges 16:28

Hannah: *"O Lord Almighty, if you will only look upon your servant's misery and remember me, and not forget your servant . . ."* 1 Samuel 1:11; *"My heart rejoices in the Lord . . . There is no one holy like the Lord; there is no one besides you; there is no Rock like our God."* 1 Samuel 2:1a, 2

The thief on the cross: *"Jesus, remember me when you come into your kingdom."* Luke 23:42

The tax collector: *"God, have mercy on me, a sinner."* Luke 18:13

Mary, the mother of Jesus: *"I am the Lord's servant . . . May it be to me as you have said"* Luke 1:38; *"My soul glorifies the Lord and my spirit rejoices in God my Savior."* 1:46

Paul: *"And this is my prayer: that your love may abound more and more in knowledge and depth of insight, so that you may be able to discern what is best and may be pure and blameless until the day of Christ . . ."* Philippians 1:9-10

Jesus: The Lord's Prayer, Matthew 6:9-13:

> *"Our Father in heaven,*
> *hallowed be your name,*
> *your kingdom come,*
> *your will be done*
> *on earth as it is in heaven.*
> *Give us today our daily bread.*
> *Forgive us our debts,*
> *As we also have forgiven our debtors.*
> *And lead us not into temptation,*
> *But deliver us from the evil one."*

12. What elements in these prayers could you use in your own prayer life?

"I have given them the glory that you gave me, that they may be one as we are one: I in them and you in me. May they be brought to complete unity to let the world know that you sent me and have loved them even as you have loved me." John 17:22-23

13. John 17 is often referred to as Jesus' High Priestly Prayer. What does Jesus focus on in His prayer?

STILLNESS

Closely related to prayer is the need for rest, for times of quiet, silence, and meditation. Why is this important? Not only does stillness cultivate an attitude of prayer, but it is healthy for the body and the spirit. It helps us to hear our own thoughts and to hear Him. God ordained rest from the very beginning. *"So on the seventh day he rested from all his work . . . he rested from all the work of creating that he had done"* (Genesis 2:2, 3). If God rested, how much more do we need rest? After the loss of a loved one, your schedule will be seriously disrupted. The physical and emotional consequences of stress will take a toll on you. You may find it difficult to sleep. Your mind may race in a hundred directions, or you may find it difficult to think clearly. Turn to Scripture to discover what God has to say about stillness, whether it be rest, meditation (reflection), quiet, or even silence.

"Be still, and know that I am God; I will be exalted among the nations, I will be exalted in the earth." Psalm 46:10

"Meditate in your heart upon your bed, and be still." Psalm 4:4b NASB

Streams in the Desert includes this beautiful passage on stillness:

When we are tempted to faint under affliction, God's message to us is not, "Be strong and of good courage," for He knows our strength and courage have fled away. But it is that sweet word, "Be still, and know that I am God." Hudson Taylor was so feeble in the closing months of his life that he wrote a dear friend: "I am so weak I cannot write; I cannot read my Bible; I cannot even pray. I can only be still in God's arms like a little child, and trust."[11]

14. How can stillness be relevant in your life?

MEDITATION

"But his delight is in the law of the Lord, and on his law he meditates day and night. He is like a tree planted by streams of water . . ." Psalm 1:2-3a

"May the words of my mouth and the meditation of my heart be pleasing in your sight, O Lord, my Rock and my Redeemer." Psalm 19:14

"My mouth shall speak wisdom; the meditation of my heart shall be understanding." Psalm 49:3

"I shall remember the deeds of the Lord; Surely I will remember Thy wonders of old. I will meditate on all Thy work, And muse on Thy deeds." Psalm 77:11-12 NASB

"May my meditation be pleasing to him, as I rejoice in the Lord." Psalm 104:34

"Oh, how I love your law! I meditate on it all day long. Your commands make me wiser than my enemies, for they are ever with me. I have more insight than all my teachers, for I meditate on your statutes." Psalm 119:97-99

"Meditate upon these things; give thyself wholly to them; that thy profiting may appear to all." 1 Timothy 4:15 KJV

"Do not let this Book of the Law depart from your mouth; meditate on it day and night, so that you may be careful to do everything written in it. Then you will be prosperous and successful." Joshua 1:8

15. From what you've read in the above Scriptures, why do you think meditation is important?

QUIET

"Then they were glad because they had quiet, and he brought them to their desired haven." Psalm 107:30 RSV

"In repentance and rest is your salvation, in quietness and trust is your strength . . ." Isaiah 30:15

"[17] The fruit of righteousness will be peace; the effect of righteousness will be quietness and confidence forever. [18] My people will live in peaceful dwelling places, in secure homes, in undisturbed places of rest." Isaiah 32:17-18

> *"Make it your ambition to lead a quiet life, to mind your own business and to work with your hands, just as we told you . . ."* 1 Thessalonians 4:11-12

> *"Instead, it should be that of your inner self, the unfading beauty of a gentle and quiet spirit, which is of great worth in God's sight."* 1 Peter 3:4

16. According to Isaiah 30:15, what do we get from quietness?

17. According to Isaiah 32:17, what are the results of righteousness (righteous living)?

SUMMARY

If you are praying in accordance with God's will, He will hear you. What does that mean? Second Chronicles 7:14 gives us His parameters: *"If my people, who are called by my name, will humble themselves and pray and seek my face and turn from their wicked ways, then will I hear from heaven and will forgive their sin and will heal their land."*

James 5:16b stresses, *"The prayer of a righteous man* [or woman] *is powerful and effective."* A righteous life produces the fruit of peace, quietness, and confidence (Isaiah 32:17). Peace and quietness are necessary to frame your conversations with God. This gives you confidence to lay before God everything that is on your heart. Can you see the beautiful cycle here: righteousness . . . quiet . . . prayer . . . righteousness?

> Prayer is the soul's sincere desire, uttered or unexpressed,
> The motion of a hidden fire
> That trembles in the breast.
>
> Prayer is the burden of a sigh,
> The falling of a tear;
> The upward glancing of an eye
>
> When none but God is near.[12]

James Montgomery

Prayer is about you and God. And that is where you are right now. He wants you. You need Him.

> *"Pray continually."*
> 1 Thessalonians 5:17

"Let our souls live in a private monastery, in an attitude of contemplation that helps us see that all of life is sacred."

Larry Crabb

CHAPTER 10

FORGIVING

"Bear with each other and forgive whatever grievances you may have against one another. Forgive as the Lord forgave you."
Colossians 3:13

INTRODUCTION

Something I now say every day is: "Nothing but love. Everything forgiven."

I have determined that to enter each day, I need to release any bad feelings before going forward, and then only to take love in my heart wherever I go. Not that I always do, but it is a good thing to tell (teach) myself every day. Remember, love is the only eternal transportable thing that matters.

THINKING IT OVER

1. Are you unable to forgive someone or something that has hurt you?

2. Do you feel that even if you could forgive, it would be impossible to forget the hurt?

3. Do you think forgiveness is important for your healing process?

THINKING IN DEPTH

The Greek word for forgiveness means to release. Nancy LeSourd says forgiveness releases us from bitterness and releases blessings to us.[1] Forgiveness withheld is bitterness held. In the chapter on feelings, you read what bitterness can do to you. There are no healthy relationships without forgiveness. Read what some others have to say about forgiveness:

> "Forgiveness
> is not only
> important, it
> is commanded."
>
> **Unknown**

- "Forgiveness isn't just pretending that what happened wasn't so bad after all . . . Forgiveness is letting go of the need to get even and releasing the right to judge, leaving that right to God." Author unknown

- "All forgiveness is really healing of the past. It is a letting go and letting God be God. True forgiveness is choosing to forget in spite of remembering. There is no demand in forgiveness. There is only release." Author unknown

- "Forgiving people lets God run the universe."[2] Gerald Sittser

- "Forgiveness is more a process than an event. Though forgiveness may not have an ending, it has a beginning."[3] Sittser

- "Forgiveness is an act of faith. I am trusting that God is a better justice-maker than I am."[4] Philip Yancey

- "Not to forgive imprisons me in the past and locks out all potential for change."[5] Yancey

- "Forgiveness offers a way out. It does not settle all questions of blame and fairness."[6] Yancey

- "Without forgiveness, bitterness is all that is left."[7] Max Lucado

Ravi Zacharias sees forgiveness as a "starting point for rebuilding one's own life."[8] That should strike a chord with those grappling with the new life of widowhood.

> *"Forgive us our debts, as we also have forgiven our debtors."* Matthew 6:12

> *"For if you forgive men when they sin against you, your heavenly Father will also forgive you. But if you do not forgive men their sins, your Father will not forgive your sins."* Matthew 6:14-15

> *"So in everything, do to others what you would have them do to you, for this sums up the Law and the Prophets."* Matthew 7:12

1. Is there a cause-and-effect relationship implied in Matthew 6:12, 14-15?

2. What do you think Jesus meant when He said the Golden Rule of Matthew 7:12 sums up the Scriptures?

"Therefore, if you are offering your gift at the altar and there remember that your brother has something against you, leave your gift there in front of the altar. First go and be reconciled to your brother; then come and offer your gift." Matthew 5:23-24

"But I tell you: Love your enemies and pray for those who persecute you . . ." Matthew 5:44

3. What does Matthew 5:23-24 teach you about forgiveness?

4. What does Matthew 5:44 teach you about forgiveness?

"Bear with each other and forgive whatever grievances you may have against one another. Forgive as the Lord forgave you." Colossians 3:13

5. According to Colossians 3:13:

    a. What should we forgive?

    b. How should we forgive?

"And when you stand praying, if you hold anything against anyone, forgive him, so that your Father in heaven may forgive you your sins." Mark 11:25

6. According to Mark 11:25, why should we forgive?

> "Forgiveness isn't just pretending that what happened wasn't so bad after all . . . Forgiveness is letting go of the need to get even and releasing the right to judge, leaving that right to God."
>
> **Unknown**

Forgiving is an aspect of love. Psychologist Archibald Hart said, "Forgiveness is surrendering my right to hurt you back."[9] I am not a better person if I forgive; I am only better for it.

You will not handle everything well, and others will not either. You will need grace from others, and they will need grace and forgiveness from you.

You will need to forgive:

    a. your loved one for leaving (dying)

    b. yourself for your thoughts of anger or regrets

    c. others for not doing _____
                                        (You fill in the blank.)

    d. others for doing _____
                                    (You fill in the blank.)

> "Forgiveness saves the expense of anger, the cost of hatred, the waste of spirits."
>
> **The Megiddo Message**

7. Why do you think surrendering is such an important part of forgiveness? What are you surrendering? What are you holding on to that you need to surrender?

8. What do you need to forgive?

9. Whom do you need to forgive?

FORGIVENESS: AN ATTITUDE

"Be kind to one another, tenderhearted, forgiving each other, just as God in Christ also has forgiven you." Ephesians 4:32 NASB

Forgiving people are gracious people. Gracious people don't necessarily want to be where they are or doing what they are doing, but they don't let that stop them from blessing and enjoying others. Gracious people always act—and it seems to be genuine—as if there is no other place they would rather be or nothing else they would rather be doing. Forgiving people understand that they need forgiveness too. Forgiving people have a forgiving attitude that pervades all areas and circumstances of their lives.

Martin Luther King, Jr. said so eloquently, "Forgiveness is not an occasional act; it is a permanent attitude."[10] Forgiveness is the best gift you can give to someone, and it's also the best present for yourself.

10. How important do you think forgiveness is?

> *"Jesus said, 'Father, forgive them, for they do not know what they are doing.' "*
> Luke 23:34a

11. What was Jesus' example to us on the cross in Luke 23:34a?

12. How can you cultivate an attitude of forgiveness in your life?

THE REST OF THE STORY

You thought you knew him so well. It wasn't until after his death that you learned things about him you previously didn't know.

Does that sound familiar? As a widow, you need to be prepared for surprises. You should expect surprises. In fact, you can count on them. If you are forewarned, they won't be as "surprising." You never can know everything about a person, not even the person to whom you are most devoted.

Some of these surprises will delight you. Perhaps as you sorted through his things, you came across a letter you had written him years ago, a letter he still carried with him in his briefcase—obviously something he treasured. Other surprises may disappoint you. You don't know where he filed the insurance policies, making an already difficult time even more troublesome for you. Or, someone tells you something you didn't want to hear.

Many widows have told me how blessed they are when people share with them the wonderful things their husbands did—things they never knew. On the other hand, people can be callous and petty and mean. Expect the unexpected. People will share with you their inside wonders or their internal garbage. Your task is to savor the good and discard the bad. You are the beneficiary. Forgive where needed and be blessed when rewarded. You have a choice. Will you choose disillusionment and disappointment, or discovery and delight?

13. Have you been able to savor the good and discard the bad in the discoveries you've made since your husband's death?

These surprises are all part of seeing the whole picture about your loved one, from beginning to end, the completed masterpiece. This picture may have some flaws, but all great works do. It is an awesome privilege to be on the inside of someone's life and to be able to see the "rest of the story," as Paul Harvey would put it.

Everybody's life is a work of art, like a painting. Like a painting, you may enjoy watching the artist at work on a particular project. It may appear to be complete to you, but it's never complete until the artist signs his or her name. When a person's life is over, God signs His name and says it's complete. (See Acts 13:36.) Just as love doesn't end with death, your relationship doesn't end either. Not surprisingly, successful living and healthy closure often involve forgiveness.

SUMMARY

"Father, forgive them, for they do not know what they are doing" (Luke 23:34). In the throes of agony, Jesus forgave those who crucified Him—even though they had no idea they needed forgiveness. Gracious and forgiving, He was more concerned for them than He was for himself. That beautiful gesture has spanned the centuries. Think of it: Jesus saw ahead to the time when you and I would need forgiveness. Can we do any less for those we need to forgive? And that person may be yourself.

> *"Be kind and compassionate to one another,*
> *forgiving each other,*
> *just as in Christ God forgave you."*
> Ephesians 4:32

CHAPTER 11

APPRECIATING

*"Give thanks in all circumstances, for this is
God's will for you in Christ Jesus."*
1 Thessalonians 5:18

INTRODUCTION

"An attitude of gratitude" may be missing in your life right now. You feel you have
nothing to be grateful for. But, if you lose heart after suffering loss, you lose vitality.
Vitality of life is reflected in a grateful heart.

The most miserable people I see are ungrateful and complaining. The happiest people I see
are grateful, regardless of their circumstances. Which attitude do you see in your life?

THINKING IT OVER

1. What does gratitude have to do with recovery?

2. Has what you're thankful for changed since the death of your loved one?

3. Is it hard for you to feel grateful when you are in such pain?

THINKING IN DEPTH

If forgiveness is the starting point for rebuilding your life, then gratitude must offer the building blocks for recovery. Read what some others have said about thankfulness.

- "Unthankfulness is one of the cruelest expressions of human selfishness, according to Shakespeare's play, *As You Like It.*"[1] Derek Thomas

- "Everyone, almost, can be thankful in prosperity, but a true saint can be thankful in adversity."[2] Thomas Watson

- "And so there is love implied in thankfulness. True thankfulness is no other than the exercise of love to God on occasion of his goodness to us . . ."[3] Jonathan Edwards

- "Gratitude is closely related to love."[4] Kenneth Boa

- "Gratitude as a discipline involves a conscious choice."[5] Henri Nouwen

- "Thanks are the highest form of thought."[6] G. K. Chesterton

1. What do these quotes reveal to you about thanksgiving?

2. Have you ever thought of gratitude as a discipline? Why or why not?

3. How are gratitude and love related?

4. What do these Scriptures tell you about thankfulness?

    "But thanks be to God! He gives us the victory through our Lord Jesus Christ."
    1 Corinthians 15:57

    a.

    "This service that you perform is not only supplying the needs of God's people but is also overflowing in many expressions of thanks to God." 2 Corinthians 9:12

"One act of thanksgiving when things go wrong with us is worth one thousand thank-you's when things are agreeable to our inclination."

Attributed to John of Avila

b.

"He who regards one day as special, does so to the Lord. He who eats meat, eats to the Lord, for he gives thanks to God; and he who abstains, does so to the Lord and gives thanks to God." Romans 14:6

c.

"Always giving thanks to God the Father for everything, in the name of our Lord Jesus Christ." Ephesians 5:20

d.

"Give thanks in all circumstances, for this is God's will for you in Christ Jesus." 1 Thessalonians 5:18

e.

"We ought always to thank God for you, brothers, and rightly so, because your faith is growing more and more, and the love every one of you has for each other is increasing." 2 Thessalonians 1:3

f.

"Devote yourselves to prayer, being watchful and thankful." Colossians 4:2

g.

"So then, just as you received Christ Jesus as Lord, continue to live in him, rooted and built up in him, strengthened in the faith as you were taught, and overflowing with thankfulness." Colossians 2:7

h.

"Do not be anxious about anything, but in everything, by prayer and petition, with thanksgiving, present your requests to God." Philippians 4:6

i.

"Sacrifice thank offerings to God, fulfill your vows to the Most High." Psalm 50:14

"Let them sacrifice thank offerings and tell of his works with songs of joy." Psalm 107:22

"I will sacrifice a thank offering to you and call on the name of the Lord."
Psalm 116:17

j.

5. Read Psalm 136, a litany of thanksgiving. What verse is repeated over and over? How does that verse relate to thanksgiving?

It is interesting in Psalms 50, 107, and 116 quoted above, that sacrifice plays a part in the thank offerings. We no longer sacrifice as the ancient Israelites did. However, the idea of offering up something valuable—something that was difficult to part with—was an important part of the thank offering itself.

Is it a sacrifice for you to be grateful, especially when you are seeing the world through the lens of sorrow? Is it difficult for you to part with your anger, resentment, bitterness, anxiety, or some other obstacle to gratitude? Just as there are obstacles and hindrances to prayer (as we saw in Chapter 9), there are also obstacles to grateful hearts. I think one of the best roads to recovery is the road of gratitude. Gratitude leads to joy. Grateful people may not always be happy, but they emanate the joy of the Lord. Remember that happiness is based on circumstances. Joy goes deeper; it taps the wellspring of God's strength.

6. Do you agree that grateful people are more enjoyable to be around? Why?

7. Are you happier when you are grateful for what you have, even if you don't have everything you would like?

8. How can you demonstrate gratitude to those around you, even in your current circumstances?

9. Do you think you don't have anything to be grateful for? Look around. Think about it. Have you thanked God for:

    a. your life?

    b. your loved one's life?

    c. your lives together?

PRAYERS OF GRATITUDE

In the chapter on prayer, you learned that praying is a way to communicate with God, to release all your concerns to Him. You also learned that prayers do not have to be elaborate, lyrical, or lengthy to please God.

In the spaces provided below, write your personal prayers of gratitude to God.

Thank Him for life. What has special meaning for you at this time?

Thank Him for family. Who is on your heart at this time?

Thank Him for providing a place for you to live. What is something special about this place?

Thank Him for your gifts/endowments/personality. What do you most appreciate about yourself?

Thank Him for the people in your life. Who comes to mind right now?

Thank Him for the experiences in your life. Your life is unique, unlike anyone else's. God handcrafted you and prepared the road before you. Which experiences cause you to feel the deepest gratitude?

Thank Him for your education. How has that made a difference in your life?

Prayers of Gratitude: The Past

Thank God for your spouse and the time you spent together. How did your spouse make a difference in your life?

Thank Him for your heritage. How has this heritage contributed to who you are today?

Thank Him for the trouble and pain in your past and how it can be used for good.

Prayers of Gratitude: The Present

Thank God for where you are now. What changes can you see in yourself?

Thank Him for your chosen family, the one you live with now. How are they helping you to be grateful?

Thank Him for your children. How are they a gift to you?

Thank Him for your work. How is it helping you?

Thank Him for your church. How has it encouraged and enlightened you?

Thank Him for your neighbors. How have they helped during your tough times?

Prayers of Gratitude: The Future

Thank God for where He is taking you.

Thank Him for how He can work in unknown ways.

Thank Him for being your Keeper (Ps. 121:5 KJV) to the end of your days.

Thank Him for your salvation and for life with Him eternally.

GRATEFUL PEOPLE GIVE

Question 8 in this chapter asked, "How can you demonstrate gratitude to those around you, even in your current circumstances?" Your first thoughts may have been to thank those who have specifically helped you in your crisis. God wants you to do more than that.

> *"Praise be to the God and Father of our Lord Jesus Christ, the Father of compassion and the God of all comfort, who comforts us in all our troubles, so that we can comfort those in any trouble with the comfort we ourselves have received from God. For just as the sufferings of Christ flow over into our lives, so also through Christ our comfort overflows."* 2 Corinthians 1:3-5

> *"In everything, do to others what you would have them do to you, for this sums up the Law and the Prophets."* Matthew 7:12

These two Scriptures, which we used earlier in the chapters on comfort and forgiving, are a good springboard from which to launch gratitude into servitude—giving back a portion of what we have received. The following three examples demonstrate how something positive can emerge from tragic events:

- After losing her teenage daughter to a drunk driver, Candy Lightner started Mothers Against Drunk Drivers (M.A.D.D.).

- John Walsh, whose son Adam was kidnapped and brutally murdered, developed the television program *America's Most Wanted*. This program not only profiles lost children, but also helps in locating criminals-at-large.

- After losing nearly all his money in the Great Chicago Fire, and then his four daughters in a shipwreck at sea, Horatio Spafford wrote "It Is Well With My Soul." For him, sorrows truly did "like sea billows roll." He and his wife moved to Jerusalem and founded the American Colony, a group dedicated to helping the poor. His unfailing faith in God helped him turn tragedy into triumph. Through his beautiful hymn, he has comforted and inspired countless others over the years.

Romans 6:13 exhorts us to be *"instruments of righteousness,"* casting aside the things that might prevent us from being what God intended us to be. It's a hard thing to see the goal when there's a curtain of grief obscuring the way. Trusting in God's providence is the lantern that lights the way or the compass by which we set our direction.

One writer notes that Joseph had more sorrow than all the other sons of Jacob, yet it led him into a ministry of bread for all nations.[7] In the pearl, nature offers an example of how we can turn our gratitude into giving. It takes a grain of sand—an irritant—to stimulate the oyster into producing a beautiful pearl.

10. How can you give back to all those who have helped you?

11. How can you help others in their pain, even while you are still in pain yourself?

12. Read 2 Corinthians 1:3-5 at the beginning of this section above:

a. How can you comfort others?

b. Who comforts us?

c. Why does He comfort us?

13. Dr. John Henry Jowett said, "God does not comfort us to make us comfortable, but to make us comforters."[8] This statement makes me see the recycling or revolutionary aspect of comfort. What do you think?

14. How do you think you are best equipped to give? (What gifts do you have to offer?)

"Remember this: Whoever sows sparingly will also reap sparingly, and whoever sows generously will also reap generously. Each man should give what he has decided in his heart to give, not reluctantly or under compulsion, for God loves a cheerful giver. And God is able to make all grace abound to you, so that in all things at all times, having all that you need, you will abound in every good work." 2 Corinthians 9:6-8

"[10] Now he who supplies seed to the sower and bread for food will also supply and increase your store of seed and will enlarge the harvest of your righteousness. [11] You will be made rich in every way so that you can be generous on every occasion, and through us your generosity will result in thanksgiving to God . . .[13] men will praise God for the obedience that accompanies your confession of the gospel of Christ, and for your generosity in sharing with them and with everyone else." 2 Corinthians 9:10-11, 13

"According to their ability they gave to the treasury for this work 61,000 drachmas of gold, 5,000 minas of silver and 100 priestly garments." Ezra 2:69

15. According to 2 Corinthians 9:6-8:

    a. Does God like a giver?

    b. How does He want us to give?

16. What will God enlarge as the result of your efforts, according to 2 Corinthians 9:10?

17. What is the result for God, as described in 2 Corinthians 9:11 and 13?

18. According to Ezra 2:69, how did those coming out of slavery/poverty give toward the rebuilding of the temple?

19. How can you give according to your ability—even in your insufficiency, even in your pain?

If God is a giver (who gives *"good gifts to those who ask him,"* Matthew 7:11) and we are created in His image, doesn't it follow that as we are conformed to His image, we would be givers too? And not just givers . . . but cheerful givers!

SUMMARY

Luke 17:11-19 tells the story of ten lepers who found Jesus, stood at a distance, and called out, *"Jesus, Master, have pity on us!"* (v. 13). Jesus sent them to the priests. *"And as they went, they were cleansed"* (v. 14). But only one of those ten men returned to thank Jesus. *"One of them, when he saw he was healed, came back, praising God in a loud voice. He threw himself at Jesus' feet and thanked him—and he was a Samaritan"* (vv. 15-16).

The loss of your spouse can feel like leprosy. You find yourself "standing at a distance," feeling like an outcast. Your world has been turned upside down and you are in pain. But Jesus is healing you even now. "Rise and go," He says. "Your faith has made you well."

But, when you are healed, will you thank Him? Throw yourself at His feet and be grateful. Jesus told that lone thanker, *"Rise and go; your faith has made you well"* (v.19). That's a good cycle to remember: pity, healing, thankfulness, rise, go, and give back.

"So then, just as you received Christ Jesus as Lord, continue to live in him,
rooted and built up in him, strengthened in the faith as you were taught,
and overflowing with thankfulness."
Colossians 2:7

CHAPTER 12

CHOOSING

"But as for me and my household, we will serve the Lord."
Joshua 24:15b

INTRODUCTION

Larry Crabb succinctly stated, "A profound encounter with pain brings us to make a choice."[1] You have reached that point. You are at a crossroads in your life. That's probably one of the reasons you are working through this Bible study. You are looking for guidance. You have decisions to make—endless decisions, painful decisions. Many options and choices confront you. You may think that you are the only one who has to make these kinds of decisions, but you are not. As we stated at the beginning of this workbook, you are not alone. Together we will look at how you can make choices that will honor God and help you on this journey.

Chapter 12 is the longest chapter in this workbook. This is where most of your decisions and daily choices are made—in your mind. Through your choices, you will heal or die daily. Let's not use the word "closure," but healing instead. There is no closure. It's never closed. It's a matter of whether you are dealing and healing, or lying and dying.

THINKING IT OVER

1. How can you be faithful in your circumstances, or in spite of them?

2. How do you keep from becoming discouraged?

3. What motivates you to persevere?

THINKING IN DEPTH

"But if serving the Lord seems undesirable to you, then choose for yourselves this day whom you will serve, whether the gods your forefathers served beyond the River, or the gods of the Amorites, in whose land you are living. But as for me and my household, we will serve the Lord." Joshua 24:15

"[19] This day I call heaven and earth as witnesses against you that I have set before you life and death, blessings and curses. Now choose life, so that you and your children may live [20] and that you may love the Lord your God, listen to his voice, and hold fast to him." Deuteronomy 30:19, 20a

1. How can God be the Lord of your life (actions) and thoughts? How do you know for sure? Would others know?

2. By choosing life, how is our relationship with God affected, according to Deuteronomy 30:20a?

"If a house is divided against itself, that house cannot stand." Mark 3:25

"No one can serve two masters. Either he will hate the one and love the other, or he will be devoted to the one and despise the other." Matthew 6:24a

3. What best serves God, division of mind/heart or singleness of mind/heart?

4. What masters you?

5. What controls your thoughts and emotions: His truth or your fears? Your disappointments or someone else's agenda or schedule?

6. Do you meet your problems with His words or with your fears/emotions?

7. What are you going to hold on to? The past (yours) or the future (His promises)?

To be active participants in life (to choose life), we have to live forward. We can't go backward. The clock moves forward, not backward.

In the last chapter on appreciation, we focused on the good things that have happened in your life. Do you realize that you can lose the good by focusing on the bad?

Making Choices

Consider the following Scriptures as they relate to decision making.

> *"Then you will understand what is right and just and fair—every good path. For wisdom will enter your heart, and knowledge will be pleasant to your soul."* Proverbs 2:9-10

> *"But solid food is for the mature, who by constant use have trained themselves to distinguish good from evil."* Hebrews 5:14

> *"Who, then, is the man that fears the Lord? He will instruct him in the way chosen for him."* Psalm 25:12

> *"Multitudes, multitudes in the valley of decision! For the day of the Lord is near in the valley of decision."* Joel 3:14

8. What do you learn about decision making in these Scriptures?

Choose Your Focus

It's the first important element in the matter of choices. What you focus on will determine the choices you make in your life. More than most people, you know that life is full of trials and tribulations. You are experiencing them right now. You also know that these are to be expected. Not even Jesus was exempt from them. Your decision will determine how you respond (with fear or faith) and that decision will determine your course.

> *"Therefore do not worry about tomorrow, for tomorrow will worry about itself. Each day has enough trouble of its own."* Matthew 6:34

Joshua urged the Israelites not to focus on the past. Jesus said not to worry about the future. Today is plenty enough for us to handle.

> "You will tend to make choices based on circumstances, pressure, and your mood at that moment."
>
> **Rick Warren**

"Do not let your thoughts alarm you or your face be pale." Daniel 5:10b NASB

As Daniel 5:10 teaches us, we are not to let our thoughts trouble us or change our countenance. King Belshazzar was so overcome with alarm that his face *"turned pale and he was so frightened that his knees knocked together and his legs gave way"* (5:6). Have you ever felt like that? Sin made Belshazzar tremble, but grief can do the same thing. It is an act of the will to put one foot in front of the other, to meet the many demands in your day, to live in spite of . . .

_____.

(You fill in the blank.)

After all the decisions you already have made, it may seem overwhelming to have to keep on making them daily. Try to see these as opportunities and not problems. With every decision, you are determining your future.

9. How are you responding to the current demands in your life? How could you respond better?

How many good things have happened in your life? Remember, you can lose the good by focusing only on the bad. It's a daily choice what you think about and focus upon.

Choose What to Remember and What to Forget

What we remember is as important as what we hold on to. It also has much to do with our focus. Jerry Bridges pointed to mankind's fickle nature when he said, "In adversity, we tend to doubt God's fatherly care, but in prosperity we tend to forget it."[2]

"I thank my God every time I remember you." Philippians 1:3

"But do not be afraid of them; remember well what the Lord your God did to Pharaoh and to all Egypt." Deuteronomy 7:18

"Remember your servants Abraham, Isaac and Jacob. Overlook the stubbornness of this people, their wickedness and their sin." Deuteronomy 9:27

"Remember that you were slaves in Egypt and the Lord your God redeemed you. That is why I give you this command today." Deuteronomy 15:15

"O Lord Almighty, if you will only look upon your servant's misery and remember me, and not forget your servant . . ." 1 Samuel 1:11

"Don't you remember that when I was with you I used to tell you these things?" 2 Thessalonians 2:5

"Brothers, I do not consider myself yet to have taken hold of it. But one thing I do: Forgetting what is behind and straining toward what is ahead, I press on . . ."
Philippians 3:13

"Praise the Lord, O my soul, and forget not all his benefits." Psalm 103:2

"Remember the wonders he has done, his miracles, and the judgments he pronounced . . . He remembers his covenant forever, the word he commanded, for a thousand generations." Psalm 105:5, 8

"(4) Remember me, O Lord, when you show favor to your people, come to my aid when you save them . . . (7) When our fathers were in Egypt, they gave no thought to your miracles; they did not remember your many kindnesses, and they rebelled by the sea, the Red Sea . . . (13) But they soon forgot what he had done and did not wait for his counsel." Psalm 106:4, 7, 13

"(49) Remember your word to your servant, for you have given me hope . . . (52) I remember your ancient laws, O Lord, and I find comfort in them . . . (55) In the night I remember your name, O Lord, and I will keep your law." Psalm 119:49, 52, 55

"O Lord, remember David and all the hardships he endured." Psalm 132:1

"I remember the days of long ago; I meditate on all your works and consider what your hands have done." Psalm 143:5

"For the sake of your name do not despise us; do not dishonor your glorious throne. Remember your covenant with us and do not break it." Jeremiah 14:21

10. After reading the Scriptures above, what are we to remember? See especially Psalm 105:5.

11. What are we to forget? See especially Philippians 3:13.

12. In several of these Scriptures, the speaker pleads with God to remember certain things. Do you think God needs to be reminded? Who needs to remember?

Our thoughts
are the results
of our choices,
or is it vice versa,
or is it both?

13. In your own life, what things do you need to remember (or hold on to) and what things (or people) do you need to let go of or release?

"Few themes in the Bible are as persistent as the call to remember."

Peter Chattaway

Choose Your Habits

We are creatures of habit. Many of our habits determine our schedules. Our schedules reflect not only what we do, but also what we value. They help to determine who we become. Many of our habits and routines centered around our loved one's habits and routines. When this pattern was disrupted, we felt like a plant that has been uprooted and transplanted into a new pot. It takes time, but eventually the plant adjusts to its new container.

When the old ways are gone, you need to form new ways. Choose better ways. Make better habits. The Roman poet Ovid said, "Habits change into character." A life made up of good habits is a good life. Unfortunately, the opposite is also true. What habits characterize your life?

14. Nathaniel Emmons said, "Habit is either the best of servants or the worst of masters."[3] Do you find this to be true in your life? What do you need to change to make your life better?

Choose to Accept Change

I know that everything has changed in your life. You may not have been in control of the changes that occurred, especially the death of your loved one. But there are things you can change about your situation now. Change is inevitable but growth is optional. Read what this passage says about the facets of change:

> Change has considerable psychological impact on the human mind. To the *fearful*, it is *threatening* because it means that things may get worse. To the *hopeful*, it is *encouraging* because things may get better. To the *confident*, it is *inspiring* because the challenge exists to make things better . . . one's character and frame of mind determine how readily he brings about change and how he reacts to change that is imposed on him.[4]

Everything changes. It does no good to fight it or deny it. Many of your choices will involve change. Are you fearful or hopeful?

15. What changes do you think would be good for you now?

16. What aspects of your character and frame of mind will play into how you plan or respond to change?

Choose the Best

If God is the center of our reality, the benchmark by which we judge life, we will seek to choose what is best.

> *"And this is my prayer: that your love may abound more and more in knowledge and depth of insight, so that you may be able to discern what is best and may be pure and blameless until the day of Christ . . ."* Philippians 1:9-10.

> *"But only one thing is needed. Mary has chosen what is better, and it will not be taken from her."* Luke 10:42

> *"This is what the Lord says—your Redeemer, the Holy One of Israel: 'I am the Lord your God, who teaches you what is best for you, who directs you in the way you should go.' "* Isaiah 48:17

> *"Do your best to present yourself to God as one approved, a workman who does not need to be ashamed and who correctly handles the word of truth."* 2 Timothy 2:15

17. According to Philippians 1:9-10, how do we know what is best?

18. Why did Jesus commend Mary in Luke 10:42?

19. According to Isaiah 48:17, what does God teach us?

20. According to 2 Timothy 2:15, what is our responsibility?

Choose to Bless

Job experienced terrible loss, and he chose to bless (and trust God) instead of heeding his wife's advice to *"curse God and die"* (2:9). God set before the people the opportunity (choice) to live in a way that would reflect cursing or blessing.

> *"However, the Lord your God would not listen to Balaam but turned the curse into a blessing for you, because the Lord your God loves you."* Deuteronomy 23:5

God wants us to choose a life that blesses. God blesses us. Will we be like Him and bless others? How can you turn this "curse" into a blessing?

21. How can you bless others, even in your current situation?

> "Cursing is a boomerang."
>
> **Madeleine L'Engle**

Choose to Live with the End in View

What will you take with you when you die? What will matter in the end? John Wesley said, "See that ye judge everything fit to be pursued or shunned, according to the influence it will have on your eternal state."[5] Read the following Scriptures and the key principles to which they point.

> *"Show me, O Lord, my life's end and the number of my days; let me know how fleeting is my life."* Psalm 39:4 [our lives are fleeting]

> *"There is a way that seems right to a man, but in the end it leads to death."* Proverbs 14:12 [our end is death]

> *"'For I know the plans I have for you,' declares the Lord, 'plans to prosper you and not to harm you, plans to give you hope and a future.'"* Jeremiah 29:11 [God plans good for us and a future]

> *"'So there is hope for your future,' declares the Lord. 'Your children will return to their own land.'"* Jeremiah 31:17 [we can have hope for the future]

> *"And surely I am with you always, to the very end of the age."* Matthew 28:20b [Jesus is with us to the end]

> *"And he will reign over the house of Jacob forever; his kingdom will never end."* Luke 1:33 [there is no end to His kingdom]

> *"Now before the feast of the Passover, when Jesus knew that his hour had come to depart out of this world to the Father, having loved his own who were in the world, he loved them to the end."* John 13:1 RSV [Jesus loved them to the end]

"Wherefore gird up the loins of your mind, be sober, and hope to the end for the grace that is to be brought unto you at the revelation of Jesus Christ." 1 Peter 1:13 KJV [keep hoping to the end]

"Let us fix our eyes on Jesus, the author and perfecter of our faith, who for the joy set before him endured the cross, scorning its shame, and sat down at the right hand of the throne of God." Hebrews 12:2 [Jesus is the author and perfecter (finisher, KJV) of our faith]

"I have fought the good fight, I have finished the race, I have kept the faith." 2 Timothy 4:7 [Paul finished the race by keeping the faith and fighting a good fight]

22. Do you live every day with the end in view? Is it easy?

Choose Not to Fear

The words "fear not" are used 365 times in the Bible. That means there is one for every day of the year. Rowland Croucher says, "Eighty-one times the Bible quotes God or Christ urging His people not to be afraid."[6] As we saw in the chapter on feelings and emotions, fear is one of the most dangerous emotions you can hold on to or cultivate—especially during this stressful time. It can undermine your faith, creating a black hole in your life that will tear away hope. Read what some others have to say about fear.

- "Courage is doing what you're afraid to do. There can be no courage unless you're scared."[7] Edward Vernon Rickenbacker

- "Fear is the greatest demotivator and emotional crippler of all time."[8] Tim and Beverly LaHaye

- "Where there is no hope there is only fear." Don Meredith

Now read the following Scriptures. Which ones can you claim?

"Only do not rebel against the Lord. And do not be afraid of the people of the land, because we will swallow them up. Their protection is gone, but the Lord is with us. Do not be afraid of them." Numbers 14:9

"Be strong and courageous. Do not be afraid or terrified because of them, for the Lord your God goes with you; he will never leave you nor forsake you." Deuteronomy 31:6

"When you go to war against your enemies and see horses and chariots and an army greater than yours, do not be afraid of them, because the Lord your God, who brought you up out of Egypt, will be with you . . . He shall say: 'Hear, O Israel, today you are going into battle against your enemies. Do not be fainthearted or afraid; do not be terrified or give way to panic before them.'" Deuteronomy 20:1, 3

> "Anything we try to hang on to here will be lost. But anything we put into God's hands will be ours for eternity."
> **Randy Alcorn**

"*But do not be afraid of them; remember well what the Lord your God did to Pharaoh and to all Egypt . . . Do not be terrified by them, for the Lord your God, who is among you, is a great and awesome God.*" Deuteronomy 7:18, 21

"*I said to you, 'I am the Lord your God; do not worship the gods of the Amorites, in whose land you live.' But you have not listened to me . . . But the Lord said to him, 'Peace! Do not be afraid. You are not going to die.'*" Judges 6:10, 23

"*'Do not be afraid,' Samuel replied. 'You have done all this evil; yet do not turn away from the Lord, but serve the Lord with all your heart.'*" 1 Samuel 12:20

"*Say to those with fearful hearts, 'Be strong, do not fear; your God will come, he will come with vengeance; with divine retribution he will come to save you.'*" Isaiah 35:4

"*You who bring good tidings to Zion, go up on a high mountain. You who bring good tidings to Jerusalem, lift up your voice with a shout, lift it up, do not be afraid; say to the towns of Judah, 'Here is your God!'*" Isaiah 40:9

"*'So do not fear, for I am with you; do not be dismayed, for I am your God. I will strengthen you and help you; I will uphold you with my righteous right hand . . . For I am the Lord, your God, who takes hold of your right hand and says to you, "Do not fear; I will help you. Do not be afraid, O worm Jacob, O little Israel, for I myself will help you," declares the Lord, your Redeemer, the Holy One of Israel.'*" Isaiah 41:10, 13-14

"*Do not be afraid, for I am with you; I will bring your children from the east and gather you from the west.*" Isaiah 43:5

"*This is what the Lord says—he who made you, who formed you in the womb, and who will help you: Do not be afraid, O Jacob, my servant, Jeshuran, whom I have chosen . . . Do not tremble, do not be afraid. Did I not proclaim this and foretell it long ago? You are my witnesses. Is there any God besides me? No, there is no other Rock; I know not one.*" Isaiah 44:2, 8

"*'But now be strong, O Zerubbabel,' declares the Lord. 'Be strong, O Joshua son of Jehozadak, the high priest. Be strong, all you people of the land,' declares the Lord, 'and work. For I am with you,' declares the Lord Almighty. 'This is what I covenanted with you when you came out of Egypt. And my Spirit remains among you. Do not fear.'*" Haggai 2:4,5

"*Ignoring what they said, Jesus told the synagogue ruler, 'Don't be afraid; just believe.'*" Mark 5:36

"*There is no fear in love, but perfect love casts out fear. For fear has to do with punishment, and he who fears is not perfected in love.*" 1 John 4:18

"Success is never final; failure is never fatal; it is courage that counts."

Attributed to Winston Churchill

23. Why should we choose not to fear? What did you learn about making the choice not to fear from the Scriptures above?

Choose Not to Be Discouraged

It is easy to lose heart, to become discouraged. Read what the Bible has to say.

> *"Be strong and courageous. Do not be terrified; do not be discouraged, for the Lord your God will be with you wherever you go."* Joshua 1:9

> *"See, the Lord your God has given you the land. Go up and take possession of it as the Lord, the God of your fathers, told you. Do not be afraid; do not be discouraged."* Deuteronomy 1:21

> *"The Lord himself goes before you and will be with you; he will never leave you nor forsake you. Do not be afraid; do not be discouraged."* Deuteronomy 31:8

> *"Then you will have success if you are careful to observe the decrees and laws that the Lord gave Moses for Israel. Be strong and courageous. Do not be afraid or discouraged."* 1 Chronicles 22:13

> *"David also said to Solomon his son, 'Be strong and courageous, and do the work. Do not be afraid or discouraged, for the Lord God, my God, is with you. He will not fail you or forsake you until all the work for the service of the temple of the Lord is finished.' "* 1 Chronicles 28:20

> *"He said: 'Listen, King Jehoshaphat and all who live in Judah and Jerusalem! This is what the Lord says to you: "Do not be afraid or discouraged because of this vast army. For the battle is not yours, but God's . . . You will not have to fight this battle. Take up your positions; stand firm and see the deliverance the Lord will give you, O Judah and Jerusalem. Do not be afraid; do not be discouraged. Go out to face them tomorrow, and the Lord will be with you." ' "* 2 Chronicles 20:15, 17

24. What did the Lord tell the Israelites in Deuteronomy 1:21?

25. What did Moses tell Joshua in Deuteronomy 31:8?

26. What did David tell the Israelites in 1 Chronicles 22:13?

27. What did David tell his son Solomon in 1 Chronicles 28:20?

28. What did the Lord tell King Jehoshaphat in 2 Chronicles 20:15 and 17?

29. What can you do to keep yourself from being discouraged?

Choose to Be Content

What does it mean to be content? Do you think you'll ever know that feeling again? Let's look at what others have said about contentment.

- "Contentment is essentially a matter of accepting from God's hand what He sends because we know that He is good and therefore it is good."[9] J. I. Packer

- "Contentment isn't denying one's feelings about unhappiness, but instead a freedom from being controlled by those feelings. It isn't pretending things are right when they are not, but instead the peace that comes from knowing that God is bigger than any problem and that He works them all out for our good . . . It isn't a feeling of well-being contingent on keeping circumstances under control, but instead a joy that exists in spite of circumstances and looks to the God who never varies."[10] Richard Swenson

- "Contentment is the product of a heart resting in God . . . Contentment is the outcome of my will being brought into subjection to the divine will. Contentment is only possible as we maintain the attitude of accepting everything that enters our lives as coming from the hand of Him who is too wise to err and too loving to cause one of His children a needless tear."[11] A. W. Pink

- "The enemy of contentment is worry."[12] Joni Eareckson Tada

- "Contentment comes from many great and small acceptances in life."[13] Tada

- "If you want to be miserable, focus on what others have and forget what God's given you. Contentment is not getting what you want; it is enjoying what you've got." Richard Daly

- "Contentment is a remedy against all our troubles, a support to all our burdens, it is the cure of care . . . Contentment is like the cork which keeps the heart up when it is sinking through discouragement . . . Contentment is a divine thing; it becomes ours not by acquisition, but infusion . . . The ground of contentment must be within thyself."[14] Watson

Now let's examine some Scriptures regarding contentment.

"I am not saying this because I am in need, for I have learned to be content whatever the circumstances. I know what it is to be in need, and I know what it is to have plenty. I have learned the secret of being content in any and every situation, whether well fed or hungry, whether living in plenty or in want." Philippians 4:11-12

30. According to Philippians 4:11-12, is contentment natural? How do we come by it?

"Keep your lives free from the love of money and be content with what you have, because God has said, 'Never will I leave you; never will I forsake you.' " Hebrews 13:5

31. What should we be content with, according to Hebrews 13:5?

"Then some soldiers asked him, 'And what should we do?' He replied, 'Don't extort money and don't accuse people falsely—be content with your pay.' " Luke 3:14

32. What does Luke 3:14 say we should be content with?

33. Why do you think God put this in His commandments? (See Exodus 20:17: You shall not covet.) [To *covet* is to want something another person has, or to want something that you don't have.]

34. After reading the quotations and Scriptures above, how would you define contentment?

Choose Not to Complain . . . or Grumble . . . or Second-Guess

It's so easy to complain. We all do it. We complain about the weather, taxes, politics, the price of gasoline . . . it almost seems to be second nature. Choosing to live by God's standards, however, mandates that we be different. Read the following quotations from others about complaining.

- "The most potent weapon against complaining or even questioning is the gift of thanksgiving."[15] Blaise Pascal

- "If the things of God were your true delight and pierced your inmost heart, you would never complain."[16] Thomas à Kempis

- "But when we complain about the weather, we are actually complaining against God who sent us our weather. We are, in fact, sinning against God."[17] Jerry Bridges

What does the Bible have to say about complaining?

> *"You turn things upside down, as if the potter were thought to be like the clay! Shall what is formed say to him who formed it, 'He did not make me'? Can the pot say of the potter, 'He knows nothing'?"* Isaiah 29:16

35. What do you learn from this illustration?

> *"Do everything without complaining or arguing . . ."* Philippians 2:14

36. According to Philippians 2:14, what should we complain about?

> *"Don't grumble against each other, brothers, or you will be judged. The Judge is standing at the door!"* James 5:9

37. What did Jesus' brother James say in James 5:9?

> *" 'Stop grumbling among yourselves,' Jesus answered."* John 6:43

38. What did Jesus say in John 6:43?

"It [love] is not rude, it is not self-seeking, it is not easily angered, it keeps no record of wrongs." 1 Corinthians 13:5

39. What does love do with wrongs, according to 1 Corinthians 13:5?

Choose to Live by Faith

Saying that we believe and acting as if we believe can sometimes be two very different things. The death of a loved one often has challenged the faith of those left behind. Ironically, this is exactly the time for which faith can do its best work. Read what others have said about faith.

- "The essence of faith is this: it gives God His place and glory as God; it allows Him free room to work, relying on Him alone; it lets God be God."[18] Andrew Murray

- "Faith is not willpower or any other kind of power. It is quite the opposite. It is rest. It is trust. It is confidence. As the Scriptures say, it is assurance and conviction."[19] Ron Blue

- "Faith isn't really faith until it's all that you're holding on to."[20] Tim Hansel

- "Trials are the food of faith."[21] Mrs. Charles E. Cowman

- "Faith that is sure of itself is not faith . . . Faith that is sure of God is the only faith there is."[22] Oswald Chambers

- "Faith is to the soul what life is to the body. Prayer is to faith what breath is to life."[23] J. C. Ryle

- "Faith is dependence upon God. And this God-dependence only begins when self-dependence ends."[24] James McConkey

- "Fear looks at the problems, faith claims the promises."[25] Rowland Croucher

- "What we need is not so much great faith in God but faith in a great God."[26] Croucher

- "In Luke 17:5, Jesus responds in effect, *'What you need isn't more faith, but using the faith you already have.'* "[27] Croucher

- "Faith is the belief that God is real and that God is good . . . It is a choice to believe that the one who made it all hasn't left it all . . . "[28] Max Lucado

> "Where faith begins, anxiety ends; where anxiety begins, faith ends."
>
> **George Müeller**

Now let's examine some Scriptures about faith.

"We live by faith, not by sight." 2 Corinthians 5:7

40. According to 2 Corinthians 5:7, what are we to live by?

Faith is not a feeling.

"For in the gospel a righteousness from God is revealed, a righteousness that is by faith from first to last, just as it is written: 'The righteous will live by faith.'" Romans 1:17 (See also Habakkuk 2:4.)

" 'But my righteous one will live by faith. And if he shrinks back, I will not be pleased with him.'" Hebrews 10:38 (See also Habakkuk 2:3, 4.)

"Clearly no one is justified before God by the law, because, 'The righteous will live by faith.'" Galatians 3:11 (See also Habakkuk 2:4.)

41. Who lives by faith, according to Romans 1:17, Hebrews 10:38, and Galatians 3:11?

"Now faith is being sure of what we hope for and certain of what we do not see." Hebrews 11:1

42. How does Hebrews 11:1 describe faith?

43. After reading the quotations and Scriptures above, how would you define faith?

His Mysterious Ways

It is trust beyond all doubting
In God who rules above!
It is obedience without question.
It is resting in His love.

It is smiling through the teardrops.
It is struggling through each test.
It is the firm belief our Father
Is a God who knoweth best!

It is knowledge He will give us
Light for each step of the way;
Grace for problems we encounter
And strength for each new day.

Lois Mae Cubel
Used by permission

Choose to Live and Love

Life is full of choices. Before, with your husband, you often conferred together before making choices. Now you have to make them alone. *"Choose for yourselves this day whom you will serve,"* Joshua told the Israelites (Joshua 24:15). *"Choose life,"* God said (Deuteronomy 30:19). The key to making the right choices can be found in both verses: 1) your choices will be dictated by whom or what you serve, and 2) your choices will determine your life.

Your feelings will sometimes get in the way. Sometimes, you can't choose what emotions will pop up, as we discussed in the chapter on feelings. However, you can choose how you will react to those emotions.

Jerry Sittser said, "Our feelings do not determine what is real, though the feelings themselves are real. We cannot ignore these feelings, but neither should we indulge them . . . acknowledge them without treating them as if they were ultimate truth. The feeling self is not the center of reality. God is the center of reality."[29]

We discussed love in Chapter 1 and will further discuss living in the following chapter. Examine your choice to live and love in the light of the following Scriptures.

> *"And so we know and rely on the love God has for us. God is love. Whoever lives in love lives in God, and God in him."* 1 John 4:16

> *"Jesus said to her, 'I am the resurrection and the life. He who believes in me will live, even though he dies.' "* John 11:25

> *"Jesus answered, 'I am the way and the truth and the life. No one comes to the Father except through me.' "* John 14:6

"As a prisoner for the Lord, then, I urge you to live a life worthy of the calling you have received." Ephesians 4:1

"Don't let anyone look down on you because you are young, but set an example for the believers in speech, in life, in love, in faith and in purity." 1 Timothy 4:12

44. God is love, according to 1 John 4:16. If we live in love, what happens?

45. John 11:25 and John 14:6 say that Christ also is what (the same word appears in both Scriptures)?

46. Ephesians 4:1 urges you to do what?

47. 1 Timothy 4:12 urges what else?

"Surely goodness and love will follow me all the days of my life, and I will dwell in the house of the Lord forever." Psalm 23:6

48. David said in Psalm 23:6 that love followed him wherever he went. Does love follow you wherever you go?

"For your love is ever before me, and I walk continually in your truth." Psalm 26:3

49. Psalm 26:3.

a. Is God's love ever before you?

b. Is your love ever before others?

"I will be glad and rejoice in your love, for you saw my affliction and knew the anguish of my soul." Psalm 31:7

50. Psalm 31:7.

    a. Do you rejoice in His love?

    b. Do others rejoice in your love?

"I do not hide your righteousness in my heart; I speak of your faithfulness and salvation. I do not conceal your love and your truth from the great assembly." Psalm 40:10

51. Psalm 40:10.

    a. Do you conceal His love?

    b. Do you conceal your love?

"Many waters cannot quench love; rivers cannot wash it away." Song of Solomon 8:7a

52. Do you let anything quench your love?

"As the Father has loved me, so have I loved you. Now remain in my love." John 15:9

53. Are you remaining in His love (see John 15:9)?

"We know that we all possess knowledge. Knowledge puffs up, but love builds up." 1 Corinthians 8:1

54. Does your love build up or tear down?

If you had children, did you ever notice that your love did not get divided as your children were born? Instead, it multiplied. Do you see that love does not diminish as you love more people? It grows!

Choose to Live with Humility

I would like to quote a great authority in my life, my mother: "Honesty is the beginning of humility."

Death brings honesty home to us: "They are dead." When you first begin to grapple with this reality, you feel fear, anger, resentment, grief—all the feelings we discussed in the chapter on emotions. But, humility? How does that fit in? Author and speaker Stephen Covey explains it this way: "Humility says, 'I am not in control.' "[30] Is nothing more evident now than that you are not in control? You know that if you could have done anything, you would have. If you had any power, you would have used it. You realize you are powerless in this situation, and this is humbling.

- "Humility is not thinking less of yourself, but thinking of yourself less." Unknown

- "Humility promotes love."[31] Jonathan Edwards

  "Now Moses was a very humble man, more humble than anyone else on the face of the earth." Numbers 12:3

  "Take my yoke upon you and learn from me, for I am gentle and humble in heart, and you will find rest for your souls." Matthew 11:29

55. Who are the examples of humility given in the above Scriptures?

    a. Numbers 12:3 _____

    b. Matthew 11:29 _____

    "If my people, who are called by my name, will humble themselves and pray and seek my face and turn from their wicked ways, then will I hear from heaven and will forgive their sin and will heal their land." 2 Chronicles 7:14

56. What does God call us to do in 2 Chronicles 7:14?

> "We are never more like Christ than when we are humble."
>
> **Skip Heitzig**

"You save the humble but bring low those whose eyes are haughty." Psalm 18:27

"He guides the humble in what is right and teaches them his way." Psalm 25:9

"For the Lord takes delight in his people; he crowns the humble with salvation." Psalm 149:4

"Humble yourselves, therefore, under God's mighty hand, that he may lift you up in due time." 1 Peter 5:6

"He mocks proud mockers but gives grace to the humble." Proverbs 3:34

57. Note what God does for the humble in each of these situations:

a. Psalm 18:27

b. Psalm 25:9

c. Psalm 149:4

d. 1 Peter 5:6

e. Proverbs 3:34

"Be completely humble and gentle; be patient, bearing with one another in love." Ephesians 4:2

58. What does Paul urge us to be in Ephesians 4:2?

"He called a little child and had him stand among them. And he said: 'I tell you the truth, unless you change and become like little children, you will never enter the kingdom of heaven. Therefore, whoever humbles himself like this child is the greatest in the kingdom of heaven.'" Matthew 18:2-4

59. What does Jesus urge us to be in Matthew 18:2-4?

"For everyone who exalts himself will be humbled, and he who humbles himself will be exalted." Luke 14:11

"I tell you that this man, rather than the other, went home justified before God. For everyone who exalts himself will be humbled, and he who humbles himself will be exalted." Luke 18:14

60. What does Jesus say will happen to the humble in Luke 14:11 and 18:14?

> "Hope infuses life with meaning. Hope is both the present realization of redemption and a joyous anticipation of its fulfillment."
>
> **Charles Carter**

Choose to Live with Hope

"Sustain me according to your promises, and I will live; do not let my hopes be dashed" (Psalm 119:116). What happens when our hopes are "dashed"? It's a frightening thought, isn't it? Did you ever wonder why 1 Corinthians 13:13 lists hope after faith? Very simply, without faith, you cannot hope. As long as you have faith in God and His providence, hope remains alive. In his song, "With Hope," Stephen Curtis Chapman sings that because we live with hope, we can die with hope.[32]

I say, "Amen to that." Living with hope makes all the difference between a life lived with purpose and a life with no meaning and no direction. But, nothing can be better than facing death confidently because you have hope.

- "Hope finds its strength in helplessness."[33] Mrs. Charles Cowman

- " 'This hope we have as an anchor of the soul, both sure and steadfast, which enters the Presence behind the veil' (Hebrews 6:19) . . . Hope is faith directed toward the future."[34] R. C. Sproul

- "Hopelessness lies in the presumption that we are actually the masters of our own fate."[35] Craig Gay

"Against all hope, Abraham in hope believed and so became the father of many nations, just as it had been said to him, 'So shall your offspring be.' " Romans 4:18

61. In Romans 4:18, Abraham "against all hope" chose what?

"Not only so, but we also rejoice in our sufferings, because we know that suffering produces perseverance; perseverance, character; and character, hope." Romans 5:3-4

62. In Romans 5:3-4, what chain of events produces what end result?

"Be joyful in hope, patient in affliction, faithful in prayer." Romans 12:12

63. According to Romans 12:12, we should be _____ in hope.

"For everything that was written in the past was written to teach us, so that through endurance and the encouragement of the Scriptures we might have hope." Romans 15:4

64. According to Romans 15:4, through what two things might we have hope?

"May the God of hope fill you with all joy and peace as you trust in him, so that you may overflow with hope by the power of the Holy Spirit." Romans 15:13

65. According to Romans 15:13, how can we overflow with hope?

"But now, Lord, what do I look for? My hope is in you." Psalm 39:7

66. According to Psalm 39:7, where is our hope?

"Why are you downcast, O my soul? Why so disturbed within me? Put your hope in God, for I will yet praise him, my Savior and my God. My soul is downcast within me; therefore I will remember you from the land of the Jordan, the heights of Hermon—from Mount Mizar . . . Why are you downcast, O my soul? Why so disturbed within me? Put your hope in God, for I will yet praise him, my Savior and my God." Psalm 42:5, 6, 11

67. Where did David say his hope was in Psalm 42:5, 6, and 11?

"The Lord delights in those who fear him, who put their hope in his unfailing love." Psalm 147:11

68. What does God do to those who put their hope in Him, according to Psalm 147:11?

Choose Joy

This may seem to be the most unreasonable request of all. You may be thinking, "Choose joy when my world has fallen apart?" Let the following thoughts and Scriptures lead you to a new understanding of this important choice.

- "Pain is inevitable, but misery is optional. We cannot avoid pain, but we can avoid joy."[36] Tim Hansel

- "Joy is not a life without tears. Joy is the experience of being loved in spite of tragedy."[37] Rowland Croucher

- "The deeper that sorrow carves into your being, the more joy you can contain."[38] Kahlil Gibran

- "Joy isn't grounded in our circumstances, it is grounded in the unchanging character of God."[39] Carolyn C. James

  "I tell you the truth, you will weep and mourn while the world rejoices. You will grieve, but your grief will turn to joy." John 16:20

69. Can sorrow be turned into joy, according to John 16:20?

  "You turned my wailing into dancing; you removed my sackcloth and clothed me with joy . . ." Psalm 30:11

70. What can grieving be changed into, according to Psalm 30:11?

  "Nehemiah said, 'Go and enjoy choice food and sweet drinks, and send some to those who have nothing prepared. This day is sacred to our Lord. Do not grieve, for the joy of the Lord is your strength.'" Nehemiah 8:10

71. According to Nehemiah 8:10, what is the source of your strength?

"For the Lord your God will bless you in all your harvest and in all the work of your hands, and your joy will be complete." Deuteronomy 16:15b

72. Who makes joy complete, according to Deuteronomy 16:15b?

"I have told you this so that my joy may be in you and that your joy may be complete." John 15:11

"Until now you have not asked for anything in my name. Ask and you will receive, and your joy will be complete." John 16:24

73. According to Jesus in John 15:11 and 16:24, how does He want you to have joy—partially or completely?

"Restore to me the joy of your salvation and grant me a willing spirit, to sustain me." Psalm 51:12

74. Do you experience joy from your salvation?

75. Before reading anything else, answer this question: Can there be joy in suffering? Paul tells us there can be. Now read Philippians, chapter 1. What do you find there related to joy?

"Instead of their shame my people will receive a double portion, and instead of disgrace they will rejoice in their inheritance; and so they will inherit a double portion in their land, and everlasting joy will be theirs." Isaiah 61:7

76. Is the joy in Isaiah 61:7 just for the "good days"?

77. Is there a link between suffering and joy? Examine the following Scriptures, then summarize your thoughts in the space at the end of this section.

"Consider it pure joy, my brothers, whenever you face trials of many kinds . . ." James 1:2

"But rejoice that you participate in the sufferings of Christ, so that you may be overjoyed when his glory is revealed." 1 Peter 4:13

"You became imitators of us and of the Lord; in spite of severe suffering, you welcomed the message with the joy given by the Holy Spirit. And so you became a model to all the believers in Macedonia and Achaia." 1 Thessalonians 1:6-7

"You sympathized with those in prison and joyfully accepted the confiscation of your property, because you knew that you yourselves had better and lasting possessions." Hebrews 10:34

"Therefore, since we are surrounded by such a great cloud of witnesses, let us throw off everything that hinders and the sin that so easily entangles, and let us run with perseverance the race marked out for us. Let us fix our eyes on Jesus, the author and perfecter of our faith, who for the joy set before him endured the cross, scorning its shame, and sat down at the right hand of the throne of God." Hebrews 12:1-2

"The apostles left the Sanhedrin, rejoicing because they had been counted worthy of suffering disgrace for the Name." Acts 5:41

"And now, brothers, we want you to know about the grace that God has given the Macedonian churches. Out of their most severe trial, their overflowing joy and their extreme poverty well up in rich generosity." 2 Corinthians 8:1, 2

"But even if I am being poured out like a drink offering on the sacrifice and service coming from your faith, I am glad and rejoice with all of you." Philippians 2:17

"Now I rejoice in what was suffered for you, and I fill up in my flesh what is still lacking in regard to Christ's afflictions, for the sake of his body, which is the church." Colossians 1:24

What are your thoughts?

Joy is my prayer for a fellow widow. She thinks since her husband died, she will not experience joy again. You know the feeling—life will not be as sweet and enjoyable. I felt the same way. But I was convicted by reading Scripture and by seeing that joy comes from the Lord, NOT from our spouses. A spouse may have been the greatest vessel or channel of joy for each of us, but not the source.

Choose Peace

True peace is not the absence of troubles, but the presence of God. The presence of God can give you peace to quell the doubts, fears, anxieties, and stress you are experiencing. What have others said about peace?

- "Peace is more than the absence of anxiety. It is a positive quality arising from inner harmony. A peace which is destroyed by external threats is no peace. God's peace, which will grow the more you understand scripture, defies uncertainty and danger."[40] John White

- "Peace is the deliberate adjustment of my life to the will of God."[41] Rowland Croucher

Let's examine peace from a scriptural perspective.

> *"You will keep in perfect peace him whose mind is steadfast, because he trusts in you. Trust in the Lord forever, for the Lord, the Lord, is the Rock eternal."* Isaiah 26:3-4

78. How do we find peace, according to Isaiah 26:3-4?

"Peace is much less a condition than a state of mind."

Unknown

"I will lie down and sleep in peace, for you alone, O Lord, make me dwell in safety." Psalm 4:8

"Now may the Lord of peace himself give you peace at all times and in every way. The Lord be with all of you." 2 Thessalonians 3:16

"Peace I leave with you; my peace I give you. I do not give to you as the world gives. Do not let your hearts be troubled and do not be afraid." John 14:27

79. Who gives peace? See Psalm 4:8, 2 Thessalonians 3:16, and John 14:27.

"Turn from evil and do good; seek peace and pursue it." Psalm 34:14

80. According to Psalm 34:14, how can we find peace?

"Let the peace of Christ rule in your hearts, since as members of one body you were called to peace. And be thankful." Colossians 3:15

81. What should we let rule our hearts, according to Colossians 3:15?

"And the peace of God, which transcends all understanding, will guard your hearts and your minds in Christ Jesus." Philippians 4:7

82. What can guard our hearts, according to Philippians 4:7?

Choose Good Friends and Good Advisors

After your husband's death, you will be left with the friends and advisors you chose together or individually. Since my husband and I had no children, I saw the friends we had made as my inheritance, our legacy. Your friends not only will comfort you, but also counsel you. Likewise, your counselors will also comfort you. The plans you made and the friendships you formed will come to bless you now.

You may have friends like Job's, who may not speak *"what is right."* (See Job 42:7.) If so, remember to pray for your friends as Job did. (See Job 42:10.)

"Plans fail for lack of counsel, but with many advisers they succeed." Proverbs 15:22

83. What does Proverbs 15:22 say about plans and advisors?

"A friend loves at all times, and a brother is born for adversity." Proverbs 17:17

"A man of many companions may come to ruin, but there is a friend who sticks closer than a brother." Proverbs 18:24

84. What do you learn from Proverbs 17:17 and 18:24?

85. What are some ways you can thank your friends for their counsel and comfort?

Choose to Persevere

Jerry Bridges said, "It is God's strength, not ours, that enables us to persevere."[42] To persevere means to persist despite opposition. Craig Gay looks at this from a different angle:

> In classical usage the term for "patience" (hypomeno) meant "to stay behind" and carried the fateful military connotation of standing one's ground and remaining steadfast in the face of the enemy, even in the face of certain defeat. The Hebrew equivalent to the Greek "await" (qawah) carried a similar military connotation, except that the virtue of staying patiently behind and remaining steadfast in the face of the enemy was conjoined with confidence in God's promised deliverance.[43]

What can you learn about perseverance from the following verses of Scripture?

". . .but he who stands firm to the end will be saved." Matthew 24:13

"All men will hate you because of me, but he who stands firm to the end will be saved." Mark 13:13

86. Who will be saved, according to Matthew 24:13 and Mark 13:13?

"Jesus replied, 'No one who puts his hand to the plow and looks back is fit for service in the kingdom of God.' " Luke 9:62

87. Are you looking back or looking forward?

"Therefore, my dear brothers, stand firm. Let nothing move you. Always give yourselves fully to the work of the Lord, because you know that your labor in the Lord is not in vain." 1 Corinthians 15:58

88. As we persevere, what should encourage us, according to 1 Corinthians 15:58?

"As you know, we consider blessed those who have persevered. You have heard of Job's perseverance and have seen what the Lord finally brought about. The Lord is full of compassion and mercy." James 5:11

89. According to James 5:11, what are those who have persevered considered to be?

"And pray in the Spirit on all occasions with all kinds of prayers and requests. With this in mind, be alert and always keep on praying for all the saints." Ephesians 6:18

90. According to Ephesians 6:18, how should we persevere?

"[6] But Christ is faithful as a son over God's house. And we are his house, if we hold on to our courage and the hope of which we boast . . . [14] We have come to share in Christ if we hold firmly till the end the confidence we had at first." Hebrews 3:6, 14

"Therefore, since we have a great high priest who has gone through the heavens, Jesus the Son of God, let us hold firmly to the faith we profess." Hebrews 4:14

"We want each of you to show this same diligence to the very end, in order to make your hope sure." Hebrews 6:11

91. What are we to hold on to, according to Hebrews 3:6, 14; 4:14; and 6:11?

a. Hebrews 3:6, 14

b. Hebrews 4:14

c. Hebrews 6:11

"Therefore, brothers, since we have confidence to enter the Most Holy Place by the blood of Jesus, by a new and living way opened for us through the curtain, that is, his body, and since we have a great priest over the house of God, let us draw near to God with a sincere heart in full assurance of faith, having our hearts sprinkled to cleanse us from a guilty conscience and having our bodies washed with pure water. Let us hold unswervingly to the hope we profess, for he who promised is faithful. And let us consider how we may spur one another on toward love and good deeds. Let us not give up meeting together, as some are in the habit of doing, but let us encourage one another and all the more as you see the Day approaching. If we deliberately keep on sinning after we have received the knowledge of the truth, no sacrifice for sins is left, but only a fearful expectation of judgment and of raging fire that will consume the enemies of God. Anyone who rejected the law of Moses died without mercy on the testimony of two or three witnesses. How much more severely do you think a man deserves to be punished who has trampled the Son of God under foot, who has treated as an unholy thing the blood of the covenant that sanctified him, and who has insulted the Spirit of grace. For we know him who said, 'It is mine to avenge; I will repay,' and again, 'The Lord will judge his people.' It is a dreadful thing to fall into the hands of the living God. Remember those earlier days after you had received the light, when you stood your ground in a great contest in the face of suffering. Sometimes you were publicly exposed to insult and persecution; at other times you stood side by side with those who were so treated. You sympathized with those in prison and joyfully accepted the confiscation of your property, because you knew that you yourselves had better and lasting possessions. So do not throw away your confidence; it will be richly rewarded. You need to persevere so that when you have done the will of God, you will receive what he has promised. For in just a very little while, 'He who is coming will come and will not delay. But my righteous ones will live by faith. And if he shrinks back, I will not be pleased with him.' But we are not of those who shrink back and are destroyed, but of those who believe and are saved." Hebrews 10:19-39

92. What are some of the things Paul exhorts us to do in Hebrews 10:19-39?

"Everything can be taken from a man but one thing: the last of the human freedoms— to choose one's attitude in any given set of circumstances . . ."

Viktor E. Frankl
Nazi concentration camp prisoner

SUMMARY

"This day I call heaven and earth as witnesses against you that I have set before you life and death, blessings and curses. Now choose life, so that you and your children may live and that you may love the Lord your God, listen to his voice, and hold fast to him."
Deuteronomy 30:19, 20a

Choose life. Love the Lord. Listen to His voice. Hold fast to Him. So many essential truths are compressed in that passage of Scripture. In this chapter, it is my hope that you have seen the importance of traveling the road of life. Along the way you will find blessings, encouragement, contentment, hope, joy, peace, and love. In spite of pain and heartache, you will learn not to complain, not to fear, not to be discouraged. You will recognize God's voice in times of trial and cling to His truth, living in faith and not by sight. In your suffering, you will know something of what Jesus experienced. And you will learn to rejoice in spite of your circumstances, knowing that God is working to complete what He began in you, for He has a plan for **you**.

"I am the Lord your God, who teaches you what is best for you,
who directs you in the way you should go."
Isaiah 48:17

CHAPTER 13

LIVING ON

"Create in me a pure heart, O God, and renew a steadfast spirit within me."
Psalm 51:10

INTRODUCTION

If you still have air in your lungs, then you still have life to live. At this moment, you may not understand why, but as a believer in Christ, you know that you were left here for a purpose. What you need to ask yourself is this: Are you going to live productively in the days left to you, or just let the days encapsulate you? If you choose to live productively, what exactly does that mean?

THINKING IT OVER

1. What does it mean for you to live productively and purposefully?

2. Now that you are a widow, how do you need to redefine your life?

3. Do you feel guilty about moving ahead—resuming a life that includes laughter and enjoyment?

In Depth

"We are to live as those ready to die."[1] These words of a Puritan chancellor almost sound like someone leading a charge into battle! As a widow, you know all too well that some days feel like a battle—it's a struggle to get up, to get going, to walk out the door and confront the world. But you must, if you are to live a productive life. Living as if you are ready to die means simply choosing to live with the end in sight, as we saw in the previous chapter.

Ravi Zacharias put it this way: "Life is to be lived at a level where the norm becomes meaningful in the light of eternal values, rather than interpreting eternal values according to what is normal for us."[2]

Enjoy every minute while you have it. You never know when life as you know it will be over. James 4:14-15 sheds some light on this subject:

> "Why, you do not even know what will happen tomorrow. What is your life? You are a mist that appears for a little while and then vanishes. Instead, you ought to say, 'If it is the Lord's will, we will live and do this or that.'"

James instructs us to live by saying, *"If it is the Lord's will, we will live and do this or that."* Don't presume upon your future, and don't presume upon the Lord. Look for His will and live in His will. According to Psalm 139:16, your days are ordained for you.

In 2 Corinthians 4:16, Paul says, *"Therefore we do not lose heart. Though outwardly we are wasting away, yet inwardly we are being renewed day by day."* Paul understood that our "outward person" was decaying daily. But he also taught us that God was renewing the "inward person" day by day.

I love Paul's prayer in Ephesians 1:18 NASB:

> "I pray that the eyes of your heart may be enlightened, so that you may know what is the hope of His calling, what are the riches of the glory of His inheritance in the saints."

1. After reading Ephesians 1:18, do you know the hope of His calling on your life?

I also love the prayer at the conclusion of Hebrews 13:20-21 NASB:

> "Now the God of peace, who brought up from the dead the great Shepherd of the sheep through the blood of the eternal covenant, even Jesus our Lord, equip you in every good thing to do His will, working in us that which is pleasing in His sight, through Jesus Christ, to whom be the glory forever and ever. Amen."

2. What are you equipped to do that would be pleasing in His sight?

". . . if you continue in your faith, established and firm, not moved from the hope held out in the gospel. This is the gospel that you heard and that has been proclaimed to every creature under heaven, and of which I, Paul, have become a servant." Colossians 1:23

3. Read Colossians 1:23 and ask yourself:

a. How can I continue to live in my faith?

b. How can I not be moved from my hope?

"But as for you, brethren, do not grow weary of doing good." 2 Thessalonians 3:13 NASB

4. How can you energize yourself so as not to grow weary?

"Do not be afraid of what you are about to suffer. I tell you, the devil will put some of you in prison to test you, and you will suffer persecution for ten days. Be faithful, even to the point of death, and I will give you the crown of life." Revelation 2:10

5. According to Revelation 2:10:

a. How long should we be faithful?

b. Then, what is our reward?

"Grieving is a process designed to help you live and love again."

Susan Zonnebelt-Smeenge & Robert Devries

Important Guidelines to Living: The "Re's"

Remembrance

As you live, **remember** what is important.

> *"Remember the wonders he has done, his miracles, and the judgments he pronounced."* 1 Chronicles 16:12

> *"I will remember the deeds of the Lord; yes, I will remember your miracles of long ago."* Psalm 77:11

6. What do you want to remember, according to 1 Chronicles 16:12 and Psalm 77:11?

Redemption

You want to **redeem** the days you have left.

> *"But God will redeem my life from the grave; he will surely take me to himself."* Psalm 49:15

> *"Praise the Lord . . . who redeems your life from the pit and crowns you with love and compassion . . ."* Psalm 103:2, 4

7. According to Psalm 49:15, how can you be redeemed?

8. According to Psalm 103:4, what can be redeemed?

Renewal

You want **renewal** in your bones and spirit.

> *"Praise the Lord . . . who satisfies your desires with good things so that your youth is renewed like the eagle's."* Psalm 103:2, 5

> *"Create in me a pure heart, O God, and renew a steadfast spirit within me."* Psalm 51:10

"But they who wait for the Lord shall renew their strength, they shall mount up with wings like eagles, they shall run and not be weary, they shall walk and not faint." Isaiah 40:31 RSV

"He saved us, not because of righteous things we had done, but because of his mercy. He saved us through the washing of rebirth and renewal by the Holy Spirit . . ." Titus 3:5

". . . to be made new in the attitude of your minds . . ." Ephesians 4:23

9. According to Psalm 103:5, can God satisfy and renew you?

10. David prayed for renewal in Psalm 51:10. What did he want God to renew?

11. What happens to those who wait for the Lord, according to Isaiah 40:31?

12. What renews us, according to Titus 3:5?

13. What needs to be renewed, according to Ephesians 4:23?

Restoration and Rebuilding

Although you want to be restored to your old life, it cannot be restored. You need to be **restored** to a right relationship with God and to others. You also need to be restored personally. Think of this as a **rebuilding** or **remodeling** process—working right where you are and using what you have.

"Restore to me the joy of your salvation and grant me a willing spirit, to sustain me." Psalm 51:12

"Restore us, O God; make your face shine upon us, that we may be saved." Psalm 80:3

"Restore us to yourself, O Lord, that we may return; renew our days as of old." Lamentations 5:21

"I will restore to you the years which the swarming locust has eaten, the hopper, the destroyer, and the cutter, my great army, which I sent among you." Joel 2:25 RSV

14. David asked for what to be restored in Psalm 51:12?

15. In being restored, what did David want, according to Psalm 80:3?

16. In Lamentations 5:21, the restoration requested was to whom and for what reason?

17. How does Joel 2:25 inspire you?

Revival

You want to be **revived**. You need reviving.

"I am exceedingly afflicted; Revive me, O Lord, according to Thy word." Psalm 119:107 NASB

"Hear my voice according to Thy lovingkindness; Revive me, O Lord, according to Thine ordinances." Psalm 119:149 NASB

18. How does Psalm 119, verses 107 and 149, say we can be revived?

"Revive me according to Thy lovingkindness, So that I may keep the testimony of Thy mouth." Psalm 119:88 NASB

19. According to Psalm 119:88:

a. How can we be revived?

b. For what reason are we revived?

"Thou, who hast shown me many troubles and distresses, Wilt revive me again, and wilt bring me up again from the depths of the earth." Psalm 71:20 NASB

20. What does David say in Psalm 71:20 about revival?

    a. Did David have troubles?

    b. Who does David say will revive him?

"Wilt Thou not Thyself revive us again, That Thy people may rejoice in Thee?" Psalm 85:6 NASB

21. According to Psalm 85:6:

    a. Can we be revived only once?

    b. Why should we be revived?

Redefinition and Reevaluation

You may need to **redefine** your life. You were once a wife. Now you are a widow. But you are still and have always been you! Use this opportunity to **reevaluate** where you are and where you are going.

"I praise you because I am fearfully and wonderfully made; your works are wonderful, I know that full well." Psalm 139:14

22. Has it ever occurred to you that you are *"fearfully and wonderfully made,"* that there are no carbon copies, no duplicates—that you are a handcrafted, custom-made creation of God? How can knowing this help you redefine your life?

" 'For I know the plans I have for you,' declares the Lord, 'Plans to prosper you and not to harm you, plans to give you hope and a future.' " Jeremiah 29:11

23. How does this help you?

Timeless Truths

Think about: **Always**

> *"And surely I am with you always, to the very end of the age."* Matthew 28:20b

> *"... always giving thanks to God the Father for everything, in the name of our Lord Jesus Christ."* Ephesians 5:20

> *"With this in mind, we constantly pray for you, that our God may count you worthy of his calling, and that by his power he may fulfill every good purpose of yours and every act prompted by your faith."* 2 Thessalonians 1:11

24. How long is Jesus with us, according to Matthew 28:20b?

25. According to Ephesians 5:20 and 2 Thessalonians 1:11, what should we be doing always?

Think about: **Forever**

26. What lasts forever, according to the following Scriptures:

> *"The Lord reigns forever; he has established his throne for judgment."* Psalm 9:7

a.

> *"But you, O Lord, sit enthroned forever; your renown endures through all generations."* Psalm 102:12

b.

> *"Give thanks to the Lord, for he is good. His love endures forever."* Psalm 136:1 (Read entire psalm.)

c.

"For the Lord is good and his love endures forever; his faithfulness continues through all generations." Psalm 100:5

d.

"Give thanks to the Lord, for he is good; his love endures forever." Psalm 107:1

e.

"Give thanks to the Lord, for he is good; his love endures forever." Psalm 118:1

f.

"Which made heaven, and earth, the sea, and all that therein is: which keepeth truth for ever." Psalm 146:6 KJV

g.

"For his merciful kindness is great toward us: and the truth of the Lord endureth for ever. Praise ye the Lord." Psalm 117:2 KJV

h.

"But the plans of the Lord stand firm forever, the purposes of his heart through all generations." Psalm 33:11

i.

"In the time of those kings, the God of heaven will set up a kingdom that will never be destroyed, nor will it be left to another people. It will crush all those kingdoms and bring them to an end, but it will itself endure forever." Daniel 2:44

j.

"After that, we who are still alive and are left will be caught up together with them in the clouds to meet the Lord in the air. And so we will be with the Lord forever." 1 Thessalonians 4:17

k.

"I know that everything God does will endure forever; nothing can be added to it and nothing taken from it. God does it so that men will revere him." Ecclesiastes 3:14

l.

"Give thanks to the Lord of hosts, For the Lord is good, For His lovingkindness is everlasting." Jeremiah 33:11

m.

Think about: **Not Always**

"I despise my life; I would not live forever. Let me alone; my days have no meaning." Job 7:16 [We will not always live.]

"For riches do not endure forever, and a crown is not secure for all generations." Proverbs 27:24 [Riches are not forever.]

27. According to Job 7:16 and Proverbs 27:24, what things will not last forever?

Think about: **Something You Cannot Lose**

"I give them eternal life, and they shall never perish; no one can snatch them out of my hand. My Father, who has given them to me, is greater than all; no one can snatch them out of my Father's hand." John 10:28-29

"If it is burned up, he will suffer loss; he himself will be saved, but only as one escaping through the flames." 1 Corinthians 3:15

" 'Jesus said to her, 'I am the resurrection and the life. He who believes in me will live, even though he dies; and whoever lives and believes in me will never die. Do you believe this?' " John 11:25-26

"Who shall separate us from the love of Christ? Shall trouble or hardship or persecution or famine or nakedness or danger or sword? As it is written: 'For your sake we face death all day long; we are considered as sheep to be slaughtered.' No, in all these things we are more than conquerors through him who loved us. For I am convinced that neither death nor life, neither angels nor demons, neither the present nor the future, nor any powers, neither height nor depth, nor anything else in all creation, will be able to separate us from the love of God that is in Christ Jesus our Lord." Romans 8:35-39

28. According to the Scriptures above, what can we not lose?

Learning How to Live from Death

Live . . .

There is a vitality to life.
There is a fleetingness to life.
There is a sacredness to life.
Life is a gift.

Live Now . . .

Life is lived in the present tense.
Life is enjoyed in moments.
Life is in the ordinary things.
Life is active and life requires stillness.
Life is lived right where you are.

Live Well . . .

by fully embracing people.
by appreciating things, not requiring them.
by accepting what you cannot change.
by contending with what you can change.
by living peacefully,
    letting go of frustration and failure,
    hanging on to fruitfulness and joy.
by living wholeheartedly,
    accepting the inevitability of death, and
    living expectantly in the light of that perspective.
by living rightly, discerning
    good and bad,
    right and wrong,
    better and best.

The Legacy of a Life Well Lived

Max Lucado said, "Blessed are those who recognize their God-given responsibilities . . . Blessed are those who know what on earth they are on earth to do and set themselves about the business of doing it."[3] Do you know one of the biggest lessons I have learned from death? It's to *live*. It's that simple!

Live while you're alive! Don't let the death of your loved one rob you of your life. It's not meant to work that way. Life is working in you. Your days are ordained. Don't miss a single one. Don't miss living each day to the fullest. Live **your** life until you have no more life to live. Your spouse may not have had a choice in when and how he died, but you certainly have a choice to make on how to live **your** life! That's a great legacy to leave—a life well lived. A life unlived is a travesty and a waste of the gifts God intended for you to use. You may be a widow, but that also means you are alive. Yes, you were left.

> "The best antidote to death is to live life well."
>
> **Dixie Johnston**
> **Fraley Keller**

But it also means you are here. While you are here, live, love, and enjoy!

"I have come that they may have life, and have it to the full." John 10:10

A Review of Key Points

As you answer the following questions, note how they review the key points of the preceding chapters:

29. How are you better equipped to live now due to the **love** you had?

30. How are you learning to live due to your **loss**?

31. How can you live **life** to the fullest in spite of your loss?

32. How has **death** changed your perspective on life?

33. How can your **feelings** and **emotions** help or cause you to live life more fully?

34. How has **grief** enabled you to live life at a deeper level?

35. How can your **coping** skills develop your living skills?

36. How have you been **strengthened** through your loss?

37. How can **praying** be more real and relevant in your life?

38. How can a **forgiving** attitude increase your enjoyment of life?

39. How can **appreciating** life enable you to give more of yourself to others?

40. How can your **choices** determine a better life for you?

41. How can you **live on** with joy and grace?

Closing Words

What were the words most often quoted during the 9/11 tragedy? "I love you." Simply that . . . those three words that embody the one eternal notion.

Choose this day whom you will serve.

Choose this day to live.

Choose this day to love.

Choose this day to give.

May the grace of God be with us all as we walk this path together.

"Love is the light—and, in the end, the only light—that can always illuminate a world grown dim and give us the courage needed to keep living . . ."

Pope Benedict XVI

CHOOSE LIFE

I must choose life
I must go on
I must choose life
I must sing this song

The days look dark and without end
The days are lonely without my best friend

But I must choose life
I must go on
I must choose life
So sing with me this song

Cause death is not the final word
Love is
Love is what I've heard
For today I choose to love and to live
I choose to love and to give

Hope, truth and love a chance
Cause this is my life's dance
To face fears of death
With grace and love's joyous breath

I must choose life
I must go on
I must choose life
I must sing this song.

Steven Gray Keller © 2002
Used by permission

EPILOGUE

to the first printing

"I have been crucified with Christ and I no longer live, but Christ lives in me."
Galatians 2:20a

After September 11, 2001, I began to write this book. My goal was to finish writing by February 3, in time for Robert's birthday. Even with the holidays and other delays, I finished on January 26, 2002.

I returned to seminary on February 12, 2002. On February 16, I had my first "joy" experience since Robert's death (October 25, 1999). I can only describe it as a feeling of pure joy. I couldn't point to any reason. I was so grateful that I experienced this, knowing it didn't come from any accomplishment or another person.

At seminary, I met a fellow student in the library who had a book I needed. We began to talk. Since we had two classes together, we began sharing meals between classes. Our discussions were great. I probed and prodded. He wrote me poetry. (The first poem was about Robert's death.) In spite of the fact that he was younger than me, I knew God had laid him on my heart in a special way and was knitting my heart to his. Repeating Galatians 2:20, I told him that I realized the Christ in me loved the Christ in him.

Thus began our love, one that was to suffer many arrows. This widow's road is a long road and you can never leave it. You have to continue living forward. You can't go back. You can't even stay the same. Nothing is constant. Nothing is eternal but love.

When I want to stay home and keep my "old life" (or go back), I realize that to love God involves loving others (Matthew 22:37-39). I choose to live—going forward.

The following year (February 3, 2003), on what would have been Robert's 50th birthday, I went to the south of France, put my feet up, and said, "Wasn't he a good one!" That was something he had instructed me to do after his death. It took over three years, but I finally made it. Another of his wishes—checked off, completed.

I sat on the porch overlooking the Mediterranean Sea and opened my Bible. I read Acts 13:36, *"For when David had served God's purpose in his own generation, he fell asleep; he was buried . . ."* And then I read Revelation 11:7, *"Now when they have finished their testimony, the beast that comes up from the Abyss will attack them, and overpower and kill them."*

I then thanked God for Robert's testimony that was finished, and for God's purpose in Robert's life—in his generation, in his family, in his friends, in his work, and also in my life. As I thanked Him for this completed work, the page turned and I realized in my mind and heart that God's purpose in my life was not over; my testimony was not complete. I then prayed for God to use my life for His purpose in my generation, and to show His testimony through the days I have left.

On my widow's walk, I am choosing to love again. I believe in the wonderful institution of marriage and the great Creator who ordained it for our good and His glory.

I have written this to unfold God's Word into your pain, to speak this truth into your wounds. This is not just my story. This is not just about me. My story is no more important than yours. My story will fade. My words will err. My work will fail. Only His story remains after 2,000 years. Only His words are sure. My story is only a way to point to His.

Dixie Fraley Keller
Orlando, Florida

Note: This poem was written by a fellow seminarian, the man I later married. I thought I would share it with you, my fellow widow.

LIKE THAT OF RUTH

There is a woman filled with grace and truth
She has a heart like that of Ruth
As the things of this world pass away
You'll persevere for a beautiful day

There's a woman filled with grace and truth
She has the perseverance like that of Ruth
In the times of darkness long
You've got to be strong

So sing along this song
Be strong and press on
As you wait patiently for the Lord
He'll incline and hear your chord

He'll lift you up out of the pit of miry clay
He'll make you fit for a brand-new day
Where many will see and hear
This new song ringing in your ear

So sing along this song
Be strong and press on
As you wait patiently for the Lord
He inclined and heard your chord

As there's a woman filled with grace and truth
She has the lovely face like that of Ruth
As the things of this world pass away
Remember, you'll persevere for a beautiful day.

ANSWER KEY TO THINKING-IN-DEPTH QUESTIONS

Note: this answer key is not for the Thinking-It-Over questions
PA=Personal Answer

CHAPTER 1: LOVING

1. God

2. Love your neighbor as yourself

3. a. Love God
   b. Love neighbor

4. Love each other

5. Love

6. He loved us

7. Because He first loved us

8. Yes

9. a. to prosper me
   b. not to harm me
   c. for hope
   d. for a future

10. As much as He loved Jesus

11. Before the creation

12. Christ died for us

13. Live a life of love; imitate God; PA

14. PA

15. PA

CHAPTER 2: LOSING

1. PA

2. PA

3. No

4. Everyone

5. a. clear minded
   b. self-controlled
   c. pray

Questions 6 - 14 PA

CHAPTER 3: LIVING

1. a. God
   b. to do good work
   c. in advance

2. God

3. Christ

4. a. number our days
   b. know how fleeting our lives are

5. PA

6. a. like a breath
   b. like a mist that vanishes

7. Eternal life is knowing God; it starts *when* we know Him

8. Those who believe in Christ

9. By His grace

10. Will not be condemned; shall never perish

11. a. Christ
    b. death and life

12. Yes

13. Keep ourselves in God's love

14. PA

15. a. faith
    b. Spirit

16. God's power

17. a. as long as life is in me
    b. speak falsehood or utter deceit
    c. integrity
    d. righteousness

18. PA

19. PA

20. PA

21. God in Christ

22. Offer ourselves to God to use our bodies as instruments of righteousness

23. PA

24. God

25. If we have the Son

26. No

27. Righteousness

28. a. keep confident
    b. persevere
    c. live by faith
    d. don't shrink back

29. As living sacrifices

30. He will give life to your mortal bodies

31. PA

32. a. use his/her gifts faithfully
    b. with the strength God provides
    c. that God may be praised

33. a. grace
    b. apportioned; different gifts to different people
    c. to prepare people for works of service, so the body of Christ may be built up
    d. mature, attaining the whole measure of the fullness of Christ

CHAPTER 4: DYING

1. No one

2. No

3. That they will die

4. No

5. a. death
   b. eternal life

6. Yes

7. No

8. a. understand
   b. evil

9. They go on to eternal life

10. They have eternal life; they will not be condemned; they cross over from death to life

11. a. living
    b. all

12. a. none
    b. whether we live or die, we are the Lord's

13. God through our Lord Jesus Christ

14. a. stand firm
    b. nothing
    c. always . . . fully

15. Once

16. a. there is an appointed time for everything
    b. yes
    c. PA

17. The hairs on your head

18. To die is gain

19. Death can produce fruit

20. PA

21. He died

22. PA

23. PA

24. His faith led to a righteous life, the memory of which lives on. Even though they are dead, their actions still speak—have a legacy.

CHAPTER 5: FEELING

1. Pain makes us conscious of God

2. In heaven there will be no more death or mourning or crying or pain

3. a. causes trouble and defiles many
   b. the grace of God

4. a. get rid of all bitterness
   b. be kind and compassionate; forgive one another

5. PA

6. a. hope
   b. God

7. PA

8. For God will be with us wherever we go

9. Don't be discouraged or afraid; be strong and courageous

10. Because God is with you and will not fail you or forsake you

11. PA

12. PA

13. PA

14. He was pressed but not crushed; perplexed but not in despair; persecuted but not abandoned; struck down but not destroyed

15. a. PA
    b. PA

16. PA

17. a. refrain from anger, turn from wrath; do not fret. Anger leads to evil.
    b. you can sin in your anger

18. Sundown/bedtime

19. Forgiveness

20. a. don't be anxious about anything
    b. an anxious heart weighs a person down

21. Present everything to God in prayer, with thanksgiving

22. PA

23. a. a righteous man is not shaken, has no fear, is steadfast and trusts in the Lord
    b. do not fret; be still before the Lord; wait for the Lord patiently
    c. cast all your anxiety on Him because He cares for you

24. Martha was worried about many things when only one thing was necessary and couldn't be taken away

25. a. don't worry about your life, what to eat, drink, wear; who can add a single hour to his life by worrying; don't worry about tomorrow; each day has enough trouble of its own
    b. don't be afraid of those who kill the body; don't be afraid; you are worth more than the sparrows.
    c. don't worry beforehand about what to say
    d. in this world you have trouble, but Christ overcame the world; in Him we can have peace

26. He did not fear evil because God was with him, comforting him

27. Don't be afraid, for your Father has been pleased to give you the kingdom

28. No

29. PA

30. PA

CHAPTER 6: GRIEVING

1. PA

2. He brings grief to us, but does not willingly seek to afflict His children; He shows compassion; His love is unfailing

3. Wise

4. There is a time to cry

5. Groaning; uncontrollable, unceasing weeping; sense of abandonment or aloneness

6. He delivers them

7. PA

8. Food/bread/nourishment/takes the place of water

9. a. He sees our tears
   b. He hears our weeping
   c. He lists our tears on a scroll; records our tears

10. Wipe away our tears

11. Yes. Christians have hope knowing Jesus rose from the dead and will raise the dead.

12. Encourage each other

13. PA

14. PA

15. PA

16. Knowing that the Lord is our strength

17. We are being renewed inwardly day by day; by keeping our eyes fixed on what is eternal

18. No

CHAPTER 7: COPING

1. a. God made me
   b. God ordained my (their) days
   c. my life is not my own
   d. man plans, God determines
   e. our steps are directed by God
   f. God predetermines
   g. God fulfills His purpose for me
   h. God has called us according to His own purposes

2. God is actively involved in my life and has a plan for me; or, PA

3. a. Hagar
   b. Abraham
   c. Ishmael
   d. Isaac
   e. Rachel

4. a. God answers
   b. answers when we call
   c. God will hear
   d. the Lord hears my weeping; He accepts my prayers
   e. He does not ignore the cry of the afflicted
   f. You hear, You encourage, You listen
   g. in my distress I can call to God and He hears
   h. He has not hidden His face; He listens
   i. He hears my cry
   j. He hears when I call out to Him
   k. I should be patient; He hears me
   l. I can call out to Him all day; He hears
   m. He listens
   n. I should have confidence that He hears
   o. He answers; He is with us; He delivers

5. PA

6. a. call on Him in truth
   b. seek Him with all your heart
   c. ask according to His will
   d. be godly and do His will

7. a. He knows me
   b. He knows what I do; He knows what I think
   c. He knows all my ways
   d. He knows what I'm going to say
   e. He is all around me—before me and behind me; He has laid His hand on me
   f. His knowledge is greater than mine

8. a. He knows the secrets of our hearts
   b. He sees my ways

9. a. He takes hold of your hand; He will keep you
   b. God's peace will guard my heart and mind
   c. He goes before you and fights for you

10. No

11. a. PA
    b. PA
    c. PA
    d. PA

12. a. God as our refuge, holding us
    b. God as a shepherd, holding us close to Him
    c. Jesus compares himself to a hen gathering her chicks

13. He is good; His love endures forever

14. God

15. Forever; through all generations

16. PA

17. Me

18. Christ

19. Endures forever

20. God, His Father

21. The Comforter, Spirit of Truth, Holy Spirit

22. a. to be with them
    b. to be with them, to strengthen and help them, to uphold them
    c. to go with them, to fight for them, to give them victory
    d. to go with them, to never leave or forsake them
    e. that His presence would go with them and give them rest

23. He said He would be with them

24. a. that God was with him
    b. they comforted him

25. Work; don't fear or be discouraged, for God is with you; He will not fail you or forsake you

26. Reminded Gideon that He was with him and told him he would defeat the enemy

27. God is with us; He delights in us; He will quiet us with His love; He will rejoice over us with singing

28. Be strong and work; God is with them

29. Be strong; God will come; He will save you

30. The grace of God

31. God will never leave you or forsake you

32. He would be with them always

33. a. God

    b. to act according to His good purpose

34. a. God
    b. to equip us to do what is pleasing to Him, so He will be glorified

35. The same God working in all

36. a. God
    b. His love completes us
    c. PA
    d. PA

37. a. obedience
    b. by the Spirit

38. PA

39. a. honor God with our bodies
    b. since God lives in us, we are the temple of the living God
    c. I know He lives with me and will be in me
    d. Christ lives in us

40. His Spirit

41. His Word; the word of Christ

42. The glorious riches of this mystery; the hope of glory [Christ in us]

43. That out of His glorious riches, He would strengthen them with power through His Spirit in their inner being; power to comprehend the love of Christ; to be filled with the fullness of God

44. Complete unity

45. The Spirit

46. PA

47. a. God prepares ahead for me
    b. who knows but that I am here for such a time as this

c. He makes my steps firm
d. God fulfills His purpose for me
e. God will fulfill His purpose for me
f. God carries out His purposes; has many plans still in store for me
g. a man plans, but God determines
h. God directs my steps beyond my understanding
i. a person's life is not his/her own
j. God knows the plans He has for me, plans to prosper me and not to harm me, plans to give me hope and a future
k. God has set purposes and foreknowledge
l. God's power and will determine beforehand what will happen
m. He determines the time and place
n. God works all things for good for those who love Him and are working for His purposes
o. He who began a good work in me will complete it

48. PA

49. PA

50. PA

CHAPTER 8: STRENGTHENING

1. Oppressed, anguish, wars/rumors of wars, distress, fears/fearful, foes, no peace, no quietness, no rest, turmoil, alarm, hard pressed, perplexed, despair, crushed, harassed, conflicts, confusion, pain, perversion

2. No

3. We can comfort others in trouble with the comfort we have received

4. God

5. PA

6. Everything He does is right and all His ways are just; He is just

7. a. for God's glory; to glorify Jesus through it (the resurrection of Lazarus)
   b. to display the work of God in his life

8. God's will cannot be thwarted or turned back

9. PA

10. Call to me and I will answer you

11. PA

12. PA

13. By the Holy Spirit

14. PA

15. Suffering produces perseverance, which produces character, which produces hope

16. a. He will be with us forever
    b. He will teach us and remind us of everything Jesus said
    c. He will testify about Jesus

17. He searches all things, even the deep things of God; He knows the thoughts of God

18. PA, but may include: they teach us to pray better; purifying; increase worthiness; opportunities to receive new blessings and deliverances

19. To turn believers away from the gospel; to hinder God's servants in their ministry; to frustrate

20. a. they are only for a little while; there are all kinds of trials; they refine our faith; they result in praise for Jesus

b. they make us commendable before God; they allow us to follow Christ's example

c. they make way for joy

d. troubles are to be expected

e. they remind us of our need to return to God and obey Him

f. they are meant to humble us, to test us so things will go well for us

g. they are meant to complete us, to make us mature

h. to show us nothing can separate us from Christ

i. they teach us to serve with humility

j. to show us we need not be dismayed

k. they are a part of being a disciple of Christ, to enter His kingdom

l. they make us hope

m. don't be surprised by them; they are not unusual (strange)

n. they allow us to participate in the sufferings of Christ; they will bring us joy

o. they are temporary; they make way for glory

p. they are temporary; heaven is eternal

21. PA

22. a. God intends it for good, to save lives

b. God disciplines us for our good, to share in His holiness, to produce righteousness and peace

c. we are perfected through suffering

d. to learn obedience

e. to learn to sympathize with the suffering of others; suffering will be rewarded; you need to persevere to receive what God has promised.

f. we are blessed if we suffer for righteousness; our reward will be great; you need to persevere to receive what God has promised

g. allows us to experience what Christ experienced. It is to be expected.

h. Christ gives us peace

i. suffering produces perseverance, character, and hope

j. allows us to share in Christ's sufferings and then in His glory

k. discipline is a part of love

l. is to be expected of those who live a godly life

m. we are never given more than we can bear

n. we suffer with the body of Christ and will rejoice with the body of Christ

o. allows us to comfort others; God comforts us in our troubles so we can comfort others.

p. we can be pressed, but not crushed; perplexed, but not in despair; persecuted, but not abandoned; struck down, but not destroyed

q. His grace is sufficient for me; His power is made perfect in my weakness

r. we are not only to believe in Him, but also to suffer for Him

s. we shouldn't be anxious, but prayerful. God's peace will transcend

t. it is better to suffer for what is good

u. we should have the same attitude as Christ; we should not be ashamed; we should commit ourselves to God; we should continue to do good

v. suffering is short lived. God Himself will restore us and make us strong

w. suffering helps us become mature and complete

23. PA

24. PA

25. The weary and the weak

26. By His word

27. Our days

28. Knowing God

29. PA

CHAPTER 9: PRAYING

1. If we obey His commands and ask according to His will, He hears us

2. Intentional

3. Sin

4. PA, but might include prayers for healing, prayers of praise, prayers for forgiveness, etc.

5. PA

6. Continually; constantly, at all times; devotedly

7. Everywhere

8. No; being watchful; wrestling in prayer; working hard in prayer

9. a. sins
   b. sin
   c. anger/disputing
   d. anxiety
   e. unforgiveness
   f. weariness
   g. fatigue; giving up

10. The Holy Spirit

11. We must pray according to God's will

12. PA

13. Unity

14. PA

15. PA

16. Strength

17. Peace, quietness, confidence

CHAPTER 10: FORGIVING

1. Yes; God treats us as we treat others

2. PA; could refer to Jesus saying to love your neighbor as yourself

3. God wants us to be reconciled with others—at peace with others—before approaching Him

4. We are supposed to love, not resent

5. a. whatever grievances you have between you
   b. as God forgave you

6. So God will forgive us

7. PA

8. PA

9. PA

10. PA

11. He prayed for the forgiveness of those who killed Him

12. PA

13. PA

CHAPTER 11: APPRECIATING

1. PA

2. PA

3. PA

4. a. thanks to God for giving us victory through Jesus

   b. the Corinthians' example of service resulted in an overflow of thanks to God

c. whether partaking or abstaining, do so for God and give thanks to Him

d. always give thanks for everything

e. always give thanks in all circumstances; it is God's will

f. we ought to always give thanks; it is right to do (for growing faith and increasing love)

g. be thankful in prayer

h. overflow with thankfulness

i. in everything, with thanksgiving, make your requests to God

j. think of giving thanks as a sacrifice to God, offer thank offerings (sacrifice), tell of His works, call on God's name

5. His love endures forever; PA

6. PA

7. PA

8. PA

9. PA

10. PA

11. PA

12. a. with the comfort we have received from God; our comfort overflows from us to them
    b. God, the Father of compassion and comfort
    c. So we can comfort others

13. PA

14. PA

15. a. yes
    b. cheerfully, not reluctantly or under compulsion

16. The harvest of your righteousness

17. So we can be generous, which will result in thanksgiving to God; men will praise God

18. According to their ability

19. PA

CHAPTER 12: CHOOSING

1. PA

2. By choosing life, we may love the Lord, listen to His voice, and hold fast to Him

3. Singleness of mind/heart

4. PA

5. PA

6. PA

7. PA

8. PA

Choose Your Focus

9. PA

Choose What to Remember and What to Forget

10. Remember everything God has done for you

11. Forget what is behind you

12. God does not have to be reminded; we do

13. PA

Choose Your Habits

14. PA

Choose to Accept Change

15. PA

16. PA

Choose the Best

17. Discernment

18. She made the better choice

19. What is best for us

20. To do your best for God

Choose to Bless

21. PA

Choose to Live With the End in View

22. PA

Choose Not to Fear

23. PA

Choose Not to Be Discouraged

24. God gives to you; you just have to possess it; do not be afraid; do not be discouraged

25. The Lord goes before you and will be with you; He won't leave you or forsake you; do not be afraid; do not be discouraged

26. You will succeed if you carefully obey; be strong and courageous; do not be afraid or discouraged

27. Be strong and courageous; do your work; do not be afraid or discouraged, for God is with you; He will not fail or forsake you

28. Do not be afraid; do not be discouraged; the battle is not yours, but God's; the Lord will be with you

29. PA

Choose to Be Content

30. No; we learn it

31. Be content with what you have

32. Be content with your pay

33. PA

34. PA

Choose Not to Complain . . . or Grumble . . . or Second-Guess

35. PA

36. Nothing

37. Don't grumble

38. Stop grumbling

39. Keeps no records

Choose to Live by Faith

40. Faith, not sight

41. The righteous

42. Being sure of what we hope for and certain of what we can't see

43. PA

Choose to Live and Love

44. We live in God and God in us

45. Life

46. Live a worthy life

47. Let your life be an example

48. PA

49. a. PA
    b. PA

50. a. PA
    b. PA

51. a. PA
    b. PA

52. PA

53. PA

54. PA

Choose to Live with Humility

55. a. Moses
    b. Christ

56. Humble ourselves, pray, seek God's face, and turn from our wicked ways

57. a. saves
    b. guides
    c. crowns
    d. lifts up
    e. gives grace

58. Humble, gentle, patient, bearing with one another in love

59. Humble like a child

60. They will be exalted

Choose to Live with Hope

61. In hope to believe

62. Suffering→perseverance→character→**hope**.

63. Joyful

64. Endurance and the encouragement of Scripture

65. By the power of the Holy Spirit

66. In God

67. In God

68. God delights in those who put their hope in Him

Choose Joy

69. Yes

70. (Dancing) Joy

71. The joy of the Lord

72. God

73. Completely

74. PA

75. PA

76. No, it is everlasting joy

77. PA

Choose Peace

78. Keep our minds on God; trust Him

79. The Lord

80. Seek peace and pursue it

81. The peace of Christ

82. The peace of God

Choose Good Friends and Good Advisors

83. Plans succeed with them and fail without them

84. PA

85. PA

Choose to Persevere

86. Those who stand firm to the end

87. PA

88. Knowing our labor in the Lord is not in vain

89. Blessed

90. Prayerfully

91. a. courage, hope, confidence
    b. the faith we profess
    c. diligence

92. Draw near to God; hold on to the hope we profess; spur one another on; continue to meet together; encourage one another; remember the early days when we "received the light"; do not throw away our confidence; do not shrink back; live by faith

CHAPTER 13: LIVING ON

1. PA

2. PA

3. a. PA
   b. PA

4. PA

5. a. until death
   b. the crown of life

6. What God has done

7. By God

8. Your life from the pit

9. Yes

10. A steadfast spirit

11. They will gain new strength; not tire, not be weary

12. The Holy Spirit

13. The attitude of your mind

14. The joy of God's salvation

15. For God's face to shine upon them; to be saved

16. To God, so that their days could be renewed

17. PA, but answer can include how the eaten years can be restored

18. According to His Word/ordinances

19. a. according to His lovingkindness
    b. that I may have a testimony

20. a. yes
    b. God would revive him

21. a. no
    b. to rejoice in Him

22. PA

23. PA

24. Always/forever

25. Giving thanks, praying

26. a. the Lord

b. the Lord
c. His love
d. His love, His faithfulness
e. His love
f. His love
g. truth
h. truth of the Lord
i. His plans and purposes
j. God's Kingdom
k. we will be with the Lord forever
l. everything God does
m. His lovingkindness

27. Our lives; riches

28. Eternal life

Questions 29 - 41. PA

SUGGESTED READING LIST

Allender, Dan B. *The Healing Path: How the Hurts in Your Past Can Lead You to a More Abundant Life.* Colorado Springs: WaterBrook Press, 2000.

Calligaro, Julie A. *The Widow's Resource.* Grosse Ile, MI: Women's Source Books, 1997.

Claypool, John R. *Tracks of a Fellow Struggler: Living and Growing through Grief.* New Orleans: Insight Press, 1995.

Crabb, Larry. *Shattered Dreams.* Colorado Springs: Waterbrook Press, 2001.

Crabb, Larry, and Dan Allender. *Hope When You're Hurting: Answers to Questions Hurting People Ask.* Grand Rapids: Zondervan, 1996.

D'Arcy, Paula. *When People Grieve: The Power of Love in the Midst of Pain.* New York: The Crossroad Publishing Co., 2005.

Davis, Verdell. *Let Me Grieve But Not Forever.* Dallas: Word, 1997.

Elliot, Elisabeth. *A Path through Suffering: Discovering the Relationship Between God's Mercy and Our Pain.* Ann Arbor, MI: Servant Publications, 1990.

Estes, Steven, and Joni Eareckson Tada. *When God Weeps.* Grand Rapids: Zondervan, 1997.

Foehner, Charlotte, and Carol Cozart. *The Widow's Handbook: A Guide for Living.* Golden, CO: Fulcrum Publishing, 1988.

Hansel, Tim. *You Gotta Keep Dancin': In the Midst of Life's Hurts, You Can Choose Joy!* Colorado Springs: ChariotVictor Publishing, 1985.

Hersh, Sharon A. *Brave Hearts: Unlocking the Courage to Love with Abandon.* Colorado Springs: WaterBrook Press, 2000.

James, Carolyn Custis. *When Life and Belief Collide.* Grand Rapids: Zondervan, 2001.

Lewis, C. S. *A Grief Observed.* New York: Bantam, 1961.

—. *The Problem of Pain.* New York: Simon and Schuster, 1996.

Meredith, Don and Sally. *Two Becoming One: Experiencing the Power of Oneness in Your Marriage.* Chicago: Moody, 1999.

Sittser, Jerry. *A Grace Disguised: How the Soul Grows through Loss.* Grand Rapids: Zondervan, 2005.

Smith, Harold Ivan. *A Decembered Grief: Living with Loss While Others Are Celebrating.* Kansas City: Beacon Hill Press, 1999.

Vanauken, Sheldon. *A Severe Mercy*. New York: Harper and Row, 1977.

Warren, Rick. *The Purpose Driven Life*. Grand Rapids: Zondervan, 2002.

Wright, H. Norman. *Recovering from Losses in Life*. Grand Rapids: Revell, 2006.

Yancey, Philip. *Where Is God When It Hurts?* Grand Rapids: Zondervan, 1977.

Ziglar, Zig. *Confessions of a Grieving Christian*. Nashville: Thomas Nelson, 1999.

Zonnebelt-Smeenge, Susan J., and Robert Devries. *Getting to the Other Side of Grief: Overcoming the Loss of a Spouse*. Grand Rapids: Baker Books, 1998.

NOTES

INTRODUCTION

1. U.S. Census Bureau, *Population Profile of the United States: 2000* (Internet Release), Chapter 18: "Keeping Up with Older Adults." Accessed 9-03-08 at http://www.census.gov/population/pop-profile/2000/chap18.pdf

2. U.S. Census Bureau (1999).

3. Ron Blue, speaking at a Crown Financial Ministries conference, 4-30-04. For more information, see http://www.crown.org

CHAPTER 1: LOVING

1. From Alfred, Lord Tennyson's eulogy, "In Memoriam A. H. H."

2. Elisabeth Elliot, "How to Simplify Your Life," *The Elisabeth Elliot Newsletter* (January/February 2000). Found at http://www.elisabethelliot.org/newsletters/2000-01-02.pdf

Also:
- C. S. Lewis, *The Four Loves* (New York: Harcourt Brace/Harvest, 1991), 121, originally published in 1960.
- Thomas à Kempis, *The Imitation of Christ.* Originally written in the 15th century.
- Helen Keller quote accessed at http://www.brainyquote.com/quotes/quotes/h/helenkelle133193.html

CHAPTER 2: LOSING

1. Brent Curtis and John Eldredge, *The Sacred Romance: Drawing Closer to the Heart of God* (Nashville: Thomas Nelson, 1997), 201.

2. Jerry Sittser, *A Grace Disguised: How the Soul Grows through Loss* (Grand Rapids: Zondervan, 2005).

3. Ibid., 9.

4. Ibid., 40-180.

5. Tim Hansel, *You Gotta Keep Dancin': In the Midst of Life's Hurts, You Can Choose Joy!* (Elgin, IL: David C. Cook/LifeJourney, 1985), 44.

6. Rick Warren, *The Purpose Driven Life* (Grand Rapids: Zondervan, 2002), 29.

Also:

- Don and Sally Meredith, *Two Becoming One: Experiencing the Power of Oneness in Your Marriage* (Chicago: Moody Press, 1999). Previously published as *Becoming One.*
- C. S. Lewis, *The Letters of C. S. Lewis to Arthur Greeves,* 20 December 1943 (Redlands, CA: C. S. Lewis Foundation), para. 5, 499.

CHAPTER 3: LIVING

- Søren Kierkegaard quote accessed at http://www.worldofquotes.com
- Warren, *The Purpose Driven Life,* 40, quoting Matthew Henry.
- Variations of the St. Augustine quote can be found on numerous websites.

CHAPTER 4: DYING

1. Ravi Zacharias, *Light in the Shadow of the Jihad: The Struggle for Truth* (Sisters, OR: Multnomah Publishers, 2002), 97.

2. Blaise Pascal, *Seeking the Face of God.* Originally written in the 17th century.

3. Ibid.

4. Ibid.

5. Ibid.

6. Thomas à Kempis, *The Imitation of Christ.*

7. Thomas Watson, *The Art of Divine Contentment* (Morgan, PA: Solo Deo Gloria Publications, 1835 edition), 180.

8. Watson, *The Lord's Prayer* (Carlisle, PA: The Banner of Truth Trust, 1993). Originally published in 1692.

9. Elisabeth Elliot, *Through Gates of Splendor,* 11th ed. (Wheaton, IL: Tyndale, 1988), 18, quoting Jim Elliot.

10. *The Closer Walk New Testament,* ed. Bruce H. Wilkinson, Calvin W. Edwards, and Paula Kirk (Atlanta: Walk Thru the Bible Minstry, 1997), 575.

Also:

- Zacharias, *Just Thinking* (Winter 2002): 10, Ravi Zacharias International Ministries (RZIM).
- St. Augustine, *Confessions,* XI, 9.
- Thomas Merton, *Love and Living* (New York: Harcourt, Inc., 1979), 97-98.
- Seventeenth-century theologian Richard Baxter wrote *A Call to the Unconverted,* a notable study of conversion.
- F. B. Meyer was a contemporary and friend of D. L. Moody.

CHAPTER 5: FEELING

1. Steven Estes and Joni Eareckson Tada, *When God Weeps* (Grand Rapids: Zondervan, 1997), 161.

2. John Piper, *Desiring God: Meditations of a Christian Hedonist* (Sisters, OR: Multnomah, 1996), 76.

3. Don Kistler. Used by permission.

4. Eugene H. Peterson, *A Long Obedience in the Same Direction: Discipleship in an Instant Society* (Downer's Grove, IL: InterVarsity, 2000), 87.

5. Zacharias, "Steadying the Soul While the Heart Is Breaking." Found at http://www.rzim.org/USA/Resources/Read/Just Thinking/JTArchives.aspx. Used by permission.

6. C. S. Lewis, *The Problem of Pain* (New York: Simon and Schuster/Touchstone, 1996), 83.

7. Hansel, *You Gotta Keep Dancin'*, 55 and 104.

8. Philip Yancey, *Disappointment with God* (Grand Rapids: Zondervan, 1998), 236, Guideposts Edition.

9. Jerry Bridges, *Transforming Grace: Living Confidently in God's Unfailing Love* (Colorado Springs: NavPress, 1991), 139.

10. Ney Bailey, "Bringing God into the Negative." Available at http://startingwithGod.com/articles/intonegative.htm

11. Billy Graham, *Unto the Hills: Thoughts for Every Day* (Dallas: Word Publishing, 1986), 56.

12. Ruth Myers, *The Satisfied Heart: 31 Days of Experiencing God's Love* (Colorado Springs: WaterBrook Press, 1999), 81.

13. Blaise Pascal, *Pensées*, XIV, 192.

14. John Claypool, *Tracks of a Fellow Struggler: Living and Growing through Grief* (San Francisco: Insight Press, 1995), 95-96.

15. Charles Swindoll, *Wisdom for the Way* (Nashville: Countryman, 2001), 25.

16. Carolyn C. James, *When Life and Belief Collide* (Grand Rapids: Zondervan, 2001), 65.

17. F. B. Meyer, *Our Daily Walk* (Scotland: Christian Focus Publications, 2003).

18. Faith Coxe Bailey, *George Müller* (Chicago: Moody Bible Institute, 1958).

19. Piper, *Ligonier* Tape of the Month 96. See also, "Battling the Unbelief of Anxiety," September 25, 1988. Available from the Resource Library at http://www.desiringgod.org

20. Margin note in the *New International Version Bible* (1995), 1810.

21. Max Lucado, *Grace for the Moment: Inspirational Thoughts for Each Day of the Year* (Nashville: Countryman, 2000), 184.

22. Oswald Chambers, "One of God's Great *Don'ts*," July 4th entry in *My Utmost for His Highest* (Grand Rapids: Discovery House Publishers, 1992). First published in the United States in 1935.

23. Jane Johnson Struck, *Today's Christian Woman* (January/February 2002): 34, quoting Dawn Hall.

Also:
- Paula D'Arcy, *When People Grieve: The Power of Love in the Midst of Pain* (New York: Crossroad Publishing, 2005), 61.
- Charles Stanley, *Beyond Bitterness* (Illinois: Victor Books, 1996).
- Skip Heitzig, *The Connection*. Found at http//:www.connectiononline.org
- Haddon W. Robinson quote found at http://www.quotationspage.com/quote/1673.html
- Corrie ten Boom quote found at http://www.worldofquotes.com/author/corrie-ten-boom/1/index.html
- Charles Spurgeon, *Cheque Book of the Bank of Faith* (England: Christian Focus Publications, 1996), 77. Originally published in the 19th century.
- Warren, *The Purpose Driven Life*, 29.
- Elisabeth Elliot quote is from a *Back to the Bible* broadcast, "Meeting Suffering with Joy." Accessed at http://www.backtothebible.org/index.php/Gateway-to-Joy/Meeting-Suffering-With-Joy.html

CHAPTER 6: GRIEVING

1. Wally Amos, *The Costco Connection* (January 2002): 15.

2. The Shiva Foundation has a Web site at http://www.goodgrief.org

3. Claypool, *Mending the Heart* (Lanham, MD: Cowley Publications, 1999), xvii.

4. An excellent resource is available at http://www.youngwidow.com

5. The Grief Recovery Institute can be accessed at http://grief-recovery.com

6. Harold Ivan Smith, *A Decembered Grief: Living with Loss While Others Are Celebrating* (Kansas City: Beacon Hill, 1999), 9, quoting Alan D. Wolfelt, who wrote the forward.

7. Elisabeth Kübler-Ross, M.D., *On Death and Dying: What the Dying Have to Teach Doctors, Nurses, Clergy, and Their Own Families* (New York: Macmillan, 1969), 38-137, 157-61.

8. Larry Crabb, *Shattered Dreams: God's Unexpected Pathway to Joy* (Colorado Springs: WaterBrook Press/Random House, 2001), 122.

9. Thomas Frantz, "Unlearning Our Prejudices in Order to Help the Bereaved," a video presentation, tape #V22004. Produced by King's College Center for Education.

10. Mrs. Charles Cowman, *Streams in the Desert* (Grand Rapids: Zondervan, 1965), 29-30.

Also:
- William Faulkner quote accessed at http://www.brainyquote.com
- Queen Elizabeth quote accessed at http://www.brainyquote.com
- C. S. Lewis, *A Grief Observed* (New York: HarperCollins Publishers, HarperCollins Edition, 2001), 60.
- D'Arcy, *When People Grieve*, 44.
- Ibid., 53.
- N. T. Wright, *For All the Saints?: Remembering the Christian Departed* (Harrisburg, PA: Morehouse Publishing, 2004), 74.

CHAPTER 7: COPING

1. Elisabeth Elliot, *The Shaping of a Christian Family* (Grand Rapids: Fleming H. Revell, 1992), 178-79. The phrase "Do the next thing" appears in the Old English as "Doe the nexte thynge."

2. Cowman, *Streams in the Desert*, 110.

3. Ibid., 73.

4. Watson, *The Art of Divine Contentment*, 142.

5. Crabb, *Shattered Dreams*, 100.

6. Zacharias, *Just Thinking* (Winter 2003): 8, RZIM.

7. Ibid.

Also:
- William Wordsworth, "Elegaic Stanzas," in *Romantic Poetry and Prose: The Oxford Anthology of English Literature*, ed. Harold Bloom and Lionel Trilling (New York: Oxford University Press, 1973), 186. Wordworth wrote this poem in 1806, a year after the tragic death of his brother John.
- Stephen Ministries offers training materials and other resources at http://www.stephenministries.org
- Zacharias, *Light in the Shadow of the Jihad*, 90-91.

CHAPTER 8: STRENGTHENING

1. J. I. Packer, *Concise Theology: A Guide to Historic Christian Beliefs* (Carol Stream, IL: Tyndale House Publishers, 2001), 54.

2. Michael S. Horton, *The Law of Perfect Freedom: Relating to God and Others through the Ten Commandments* (Chicago: Moody, 1993), 39.

3. Provided by the Christian Classics Ethereal Library (CCEL). Accessed at http://www.ccel.org/creeds/heidelberg-cat-ext.txt.

4. Ibid.

5. Crabb, *Shattered Dreams*, 98.

6. Thomas Watson, *The Beatitudes: An Exposition of Matthew 5:1-12*. Found at http://www.biblebb.com/files/TW/tw-beatitudes.htm. Watson lived from 1620-1686.

7. Elisabeth Elliot. From a presentation.

8. à Kempis, *The Imitation of Christ*.

9. R. C. Sproul, *Essential Truths of the Christian Faith* (Carol Stream, IL: Tyndale House Publishers, 1998), 31.

10. Watson, *The Beatitudes*.

11. Watson, *The Art of Divine Contentment*, 137.

12. Cowman, *Streams in the Desert*, 243.

13. Ibid., 171.

14. Pascal, *Seeking the Face of God*, 177.

15. Ibid., 170.

16. Pascal, *Letter to Monsieur and Mlle de Rouannez*, November, 1656.

17. Dr. Larry Crabb, *Finding God* (Grand Rapids: Zondervan, 1993), 38.

18. George Eldon Ladd, *A Theology of the New Testament* (Grand Rapids: Eerdmans, 1974), 440.

19. Cowman, *Streams in the Desert*, p. 314.

20. Estes and Tada, *When God Weeps*, 140, 142.

21. C. S. Lewis, *A Grief Observed*, 33.

22. Hansel, *You Gotta Keep Dancin'*, 115.

23. Elisabeth Elliot, "Suffering Is Not for Nothing." A presentation.

24. Brent Curtis and John Eldredge, *The Sacred Romance: Drawing Closer to the Heart of God* (Nashville: Thomas Nelson, Inc., 1997), 185, quoting Simone Weil.

Also:
- For information on Pastor Charles Price, visit http://www.livingtruth.ca
- Thomas Boston sidebar quotes found in Curtis I. Crenshaw, *How to Profit from Our Afflictions* (Spring, TX: Footstool Publications, 1990). Originally titled *The Crook in the Lot* by Thomas Boston.
- Charles Spurgeon's words are from his sermon, "The Throne of Grace," delivered Nov. 19, 1871. Accessed at http://www.spurgeon.org/sermons/1024.htm
- Howard G. Hendricks is a distinguished professor and chairman of the Center for Christian Leadership at Dallas Theological Seminary.
- Paul Claudel quote found at http://wordincarnate.wordpress.com/2008/08/23/jesus-wept/
- Bruce Waltke quote taken from author's class notes at his lecture
- Denise Sproul, *Every Thought Captive*, Vol. 7, Issue 2 (March/April 2003). The Publication of the Highland Study Center.
- Philip Yancey, "Living with Furious Opposites," in *The Best Christian Writing 2001*, ed. John Wilson (San Francisco: HarperCollins, 2001), 328.

CHAPTER 9: PRAYING

1. Howard G. Hendricks and William D. Hendricks, *Living by the Book* (Chicago: Moody Publisher, 1993), 99.

2. Ibid., 100.

3. Based on Oswald Chambers, *Prayer: A Holy Occupation* (Grand Rapids, MI: Discovery House, 1992), 53.

4. Chambers, *Prayer: A Holy Occupation*, 72.

5. A. W. Pink, *The Sovereignty of God* (The Banner of Truth Trust, 1988), 115.

6. Ibid., 118.

7. Henry T. Blackaby and Claude V. King, *Experiencing God: Knowing and Doing the Will of God* (Nashville: LifeWay Press, 1990), 87.

8. Watson, *The Beatitudes*, 228.

9. Madeleine L'Engle, *Glimpses of Grace: Daily Thoughts and Reflections* (New York: Harper One, 1997), 124.

10. Piper, *Desiring God*, 147.

11. Cowman, *Streams in the Desert*, 153.

12. Derek Thomas, *Making the Most of Your Devotional Life* (Darlington, England: Evangelical Press, 2001), 73, quoting James Montgomery

Also:
- John Bunyan quote from *The Pilgrim's Progress* found at http://chi.gospelcom.net Click on "Glimpses of Christian History" link.
- Crabb, *Shattered Dreams*, 101.

CHAPTER 10: FORGIVING

1. Nancy LeSourd, *No Longer the Hero: The Personal Pilgrimage of an Adult Child* (Nashville: Thomas Nelson, 1991), 203.

2. Sittser, *A Grace Disguised*, 127.

3. Ibid., 129.

4. Yancey, *What's So Amazing About Grace?* (Grand Rapids: Zondervan, 1997), 93.

5. Ibid., 99.

6. Ibid., 98.

7. Max Lucado, *The Applause of Heaven* (Dallas: Word Publishing, 1999), 113.

8. Zacharias, *Can Man Live Without God?* (Nashville: Thomas Nelson, 2004), 173.

9. Archibald D. Hart, *Thrilled to Death: How the Endless Pursuit of Pleasure is Leaving Us Numb* (Nashville: Thomas Nelson, 2007), 247.

10. Martin Luther King, Jr. quote found at http://www.betterworld.net/quotes/forgiveness-quotes-3.htm

Also:
- Quote from *The Megiddo Message* accessed at http://www.hopetriumphant.com/inspirational_quotes_a_to_f_.htm

CHAPTER 11: APPRECIATING

1. Thomas, *Making the Most of Your Devotional Life*, 207.

2. Watson, *Divine Cordial, or, The transcendent privilege of those that love God and are lovingly called . . .* First published in 1663. Accessed at ccel.org/ccel/Watson/cordial.vi.html

3. Jonathan Edwards, *Charity and Its Fruits: Or, Christian Love as Manifested in the Heart and Life* (New York: Robert Carter & Brothers, 1852), 395.

4. Kenneth Boa, *That I May Know God: Pathways to Spiritual Formation* (Sisters, OR: Multnomah, 1998), 139.

5. Henri J. M. Nouwen, *The Return of the Prodigal Son: A Story of Homecoming* (New York: Doubleday/Image, 1994), 83.

6. Dale Ahlquist, *Common Sense 101: Lessons from G. K. Chesterton* (Ft. Collins, CO: Ignatius Press, 2006), 35, quoting Chesterton.

7. Cowman, *Streams in the Desert*, 30.

8. Ibid., 19, quoting Dr. John Henry Jowett.

Also:
- John of Avila was a 16th-century preacher, author, and mystic.

CHAPTER 12: CHOOSING

1. Crabb, *Shattered Dreams*, 88.

2. Jerry Bridges, *Trusting God: Even When Life Hurts* (Colorado Springs: NavPress, 1990), 201.

3. The quote from colonial artist Nathaniel Emmons (1704-1740) can be found at http://www.famous-quotes.com/author.pkp?aid=2301

4. Mark A. Smith and Larry M. Lindsay, *Leading Change in Your World* (Marion, IN: Triangle Publishing, 2001), 4, quoting King Whitney, Jr.

5. John Wesley, "The Difference Between Walking by Sight, and Walking by Faith," accessed at http://www.new.gbgm-umc.org/umhistory/wesley/sermons/113

6. Rowland Croucher, *Sunrise, Sunset: Prayers and Meditations for Every Day of the Year* (New York: HarperCollins, 1995), 9.

7. Eddie Rickenbacker quote found at http://www.quotegarden.com/courage.html

8. Tim and Beverly LaHaye, *The Beauty of Sexual Love* (Grand Rapids: Zondervan, 1998), 179.

9. J. I. Packer, "The Secret of Contentment," an address given at Wheaton College, Wheaton, Illinois, 27 February 1984. Quoted in *Margins* by Richard Swenson, 187 (see below).

10. Richard Swenson, *Margins: Restoring Emotional, Physical, Financial, and Time Reserves to Overloaded Lives* (Colorado Springs: NavPress, 1992), 188.

11. A. W. Pink, as quoted in the *Closer Walk New Test*ament, 670.

12. Estes and Tada, *When God Weeps*, 184.

13. Ibid., 185

14. Watson, *The Art of Divine Contentment*, 104, 112, 132, 222.

15. Pascal, *Seeking the Face of God*, 89.

16. à Kempis, *The Imitation of Christ*.

17. Bridges, *Trusting God*, 96.

18. Andrew Murray, *Be Perfect* (Springdale, PA: Whitaker House, 1982), 32.

19. Ron Blue. Used by permission.

20. Hansel, *You Gotta Keep Dancin'*, 42.

21. Cowman, *Streams in the Desert*, 127.

22. Oswald Chambers quote found under the listing for *Faith: A Holy Walk* at http://www.oswaldchambers.co.uk/books.html

23. Bishop J. C. Ryle lived from 1816-1900. His sermon, "A Call to Prayer," can be accessed at http://www.anglicanlibrary.org/ryle/sermonsandtracts/calltoprayer.htm

24. Boa, *That I May Know God*, 117, quoting James McConkey.

25. Croucher, *Sunrise, Sunset*, 47.

26. Ibid.

27. Ibid., 49.

28. Lucado, *Grace for the Moment*, 70.

29. Sittser, *A Grace Disguised*, 88.

30. Stephen R. Covey, "The Strange Attractor," *Executive Excellence* (August 1994): 5-6.

31. Jonathan Edwards, "All the Graces of Christianity Connected," accessed at http://www.biblebb.com/files/edwards/charity13.htm

32. Stephen Curtis Chapman, "With Hope." 1999 Sparrow Song/Peach Hill Songs/BMI. Admin. by EMI Christian Music Publishing.

33. Cowman, *Streams in the Desert*, 104.

34. Sproul, *Essential Truths*, 59.

35. Craig M. Gay, *The Way of the Modern World: Or, Why It's Tempting to Live As If God Doesn't Exist* (Grand Rapids: Eerdmans, 1998), 75.

36. Hansel, *You Gotta Keep Dancin'*, 55.

37. Croucher, *Sunrise, Sunset*, 40.

38. Kahlil Gibran, *The Prophet* (Hertfordshire: Wordsworth Editions Ltd.UK, 1997), 16.

39. James, *When Life and Belief Collide*, 146.

40. John White, *The Fight: A Practical Handbook to Christian Living* (Downer's Grove, IL: InterVarsity, 1976), 42.

41. Croucher, *Sunrise, Sunset*, 40.

42. Bridges, *Trusting God*, 186.

43. Gay, *The Way of the Modern World*, 312.

Also:
- Peter Chattaway, *Books & Culture* (January/February 2005): 14.
- Warren, *The Purpose Driven Life*, 31.
- L'Engle, *Glimpses of Grace*, 55.
- Randy Alcorn, *The Treasure Principle: Discovering the Secret of Joyful Living* (Sisters, OR: Multonomah, 2001), 18.
- Meredith, *Two Becoming One*, 151.
- Richard Daly, *God's Little Book of Calm: Words of Peace and Refreshment for Weary Souls* (London: HarperCollins, 1999).
- George Müeller quote found at http://pinecrestbiblechurch.com/quotes.html
- Heitzig, *The Connection*. Found at http://www.connectiononline.org
- Charles Carter, gen. ed., *A Contemporary Wesleyan Theology: Biblical, Systematic, and Practical* (Grand Rapids: Zondervan, 1983).
- Viktor E. Frankl, *Man's Search for Meaning* (New York: Washington Square Press/Pocket Books, 1984), 86.

CHAPTER 13: LIVING ON

1. Thomas, *Making the Most of Your Devotional Life*, 22.

2. Zacharias, *Light in the Shadow of the Jihad*, 88.

3. Lucado, *Grace for the Moment*, 277.

Also:

- Susan J. Zonnebelt-Smeenge and Robert Devries, *Getting to the Other Side of Grief: Overcoming the Loss of a Spouse* (Grand Rapids: Baker Books, 1998), 54.
- The quote from Pope Benedict XVI is from his *First Encyclical*, January 25, 2006.

LEADER'S GUIDELINES
AND SUGGESTIONS FOR GROUP STUDIES

OVERVIEW

As a leader/facilitator in this group study, your purpose is to be an encourager, gently helping participants come up with answers to the questions in this book. You also are to be the glue, so to speak, holding the group together and preventing it from unraveling into unproductive tangents. There are no wrong answers. Some answers will be better than others. What you are looking for in group discussion is:

- full participation by all involved
- transparent/real answers, not just answers that "sound good"
- depth of insight and growth

Tell your participants that this study is for *them*! What they take out is determined by what they put in. They will benefit not only individually, but also corporately. As a leader, you will discover that every group has a unique "signature," a personality unlike any other. Part of the joy you will experience is seeing how participants connect, discover commonalities, grow together, understand one another, encourage one another, and move through their pain—together.

GETTING STARTED

We recommend that you begin and end each session with a Scripture verse and prayer. The opening prayer sets the tone for each class, preparing hearts for the journey ahead. The closing prayer pulls thematic threads together and places all concerns at the feet of Jesus.

You will notice that each chapter begins with a Scripture and ends with a Scripture, both of which are related to the theme of the chapter. These Scriptures are good choices to open and close sessions, or you may choose different verses. By quoting these verses out loud, you cement the chapter themes, as well as encourage participants to make them into memory verses. This is entirely up to you and your group. We have tried to include a variety of tools to make each session as interesting and flexible as possible.

INTRODUCTION AND THINKING IT OVER

The "Introduction" does just that—introduces the group to the chapter theme. The "Thinking It Over" section focuses on the broad brush strokes of the Introduction. These questions are not meant to take a lot of class time. They are helpful for initiating discussion or to "get the ball rolling." It is important to remember that these questions are always "*just what do* **you** *think*" questions, questions we might ask before we look at what God's Word has to say. As we seek clarity, we learn that our way of looking at situations does not always match God's way.

THINKING IN DEPTH

The essence of your group's discussion should revolve around the "Thinking in Depth" section. These questions help the participant explore the chapter topics, using the lens of Scripture.

If you have time in your group setting, you may want to read the Scriptures out loud with the questions. The more God's Word is read aloud, the more people will hear it. The more they hear it, the more they will ponder it and allow it to take up residence in their minds. The ultimate goal, of course, is for participants to engrave God's Word on their hearts (see Romans 10:17; 2 Corinthians 3:3; Jeremiah 31:33).

SUMMARY

The "Summary" section serves to polish the gold that participants have mined in their discussion of the chapter. Always remember that your participants are on a journey of discovery. Encourage them to share any additional insights they may have found in their study.

CHAPTER OVERVIEWS

Chapter One: Loving

As we suggested earlier, always start and end each session with prayer. To demonstrate the importance of Scripture in helping participants deal with their widow's journey, we encourage you to quote Scripture out loud. You might even like to do this as a class, speaking the Scripture verse out loud together.

Ideally, your group has had a chance to meet together before this first class session. We advise you to set up an orientation meeting as a way for participants to get to know one another and share their individual stories. If this is not possible, then in your first class meeting, go around the room and ask each woman to introduce herself and share a little of her experience as a widow. You might encourage participants to explain how long they have been widowed and perhaps share something of their personal stories. Depending on the size of your group, you may need to set some parameters—for example, suggest that they just speak a couple of minutes each. Remember that "sharing" cannot be forced. Some women are more at ease with this than others. Your focus is to help everyone feel comfortable and safe.

Key questions in Chapter 1 are Questions 14 and 15. It is important for your widows to really believe that God loves them and that they are better people for having loved and been loved.

This chapter metaphorically cultivates the soil, preparing you for your next meeting on the theme of loss.

As you close this session, you may quote the Scripture we have provided at the end of the chapter. Before initiating the closing prayer, do allow time for prayer requests. During your closing prayer, pray for a blessing on what you are learning together and what God will work in their hearts.

Chapter 2: Losing

Throughout this lesson, your goal is to help participants grasp the fact that loss is both universal and unique. They are not alone. Others have walked the widow's path and are able to understand what they are going through. They can offer help and can even walk with them. Still, each new widow realizes that her situation is unique to her.

This is a short lesson, but a tough one. Your participants may find this week to be a hard week. They may feel their loss anew; they may also sense a diminishing of hope. When you gather for discussion, acknowledge this. The structure of this chapter allows participants more time to talk about their loss and the changes they are experiencing. Allow them to unload and share. Be patient. This lesson helps participants come to grips with their loss. It also underscores their need to build something positive from it. We have often found that the discussion of this chapter can be very emotional, very revealing—and also a wonderful time of bonding.

Chapter 3: Living

In this chapter, you will help participants look at life and its meaning. Essentially, this means distinguishing the difference between an earthly perspective and an eternal perspective. In examining this difference, you will show them how an eternal perspective affects the quality and uniqueness of life. Draw a parallel to what they discovered in Chapter 2—that loss can diminish hope or reinvigorate it. The choice is theirs.

Chapter 4: Dying

Studying death is not easy. Your participants know death "up close and personal." In this chapter, we look in a general way at the subject of death and ponder its implications—one of which is its inevitability.

As you may have discovered, our overall pattern is to balance chapter themes. Thus, you may hear participants say they had a "good week," followed by a "sad week." The topics set the tone: Love followed by Loss; Life followed by Death. This is meant to pace your group, but also to keep them moving. Widows need to reflect on all of these issues.

Each participant should grasp fully that we all will die. Although each death is unique, it is unavoidable and inevitable. Death is the final chapter in our earthly life, but it does not have the final word. Help your participants realize the hope they have in Jesus Christ. Help them know that even in death, they are never alone.

Chapter 5: Feeling

The death of a spouse may introduce feelings the surviving spouse has not experienced before. This chapter covers a lot of territory! You also will find that a lot will come out in discussion. You may want to address each topic (pain, bitterness, resentment, disappointment, etc.) and ask which ones the participants most identify with, or you may discuss other related topics. Establish early in the discussion that these kinds of feelings are a natural response to loss. Validate your participants' feelings and allow them to express themselves freely. However, help them realize that feelings cannot substitute for reality. Left unchecked, feelings will drain them and prevent them from living by God's truth.

Chapter 6: Grieving

Grieving is a process. Everyone grieves differently, but grief is universal. As you lead the discussion, demonstrate through Scripture that even great biblical personalities were not immune to grief. Help participants understand the stages of grief and ask for their input on how they have worked through these various stages. Your goal is to help them understand that it is "okay" to grieve. Let them know that in your group they are safe to share what they have experienced. Underscore that each of them may be at a different level in the grieving process. By sharing their experiences, they help one another and grow together.

Chapter 7: Coping

This is one of the longest chapters, but it captures the essence of what this book is about: where widows find themselves in their journey, and what they need as they travel this difficult path. Because we have included so many Scriptures, we suggest that you condense these to a few pivotal verses under each subheading. As time permits, ask participants for a summary of what they learned under each subheading. For example, with Question 4, ask participants to offer the basic lessons they learned from the verses, rather than read every Scripture. However, emphasize that for their overall spiritual growth, they should not cut corners. Encourage them to read all the Scriptures on their own time and make notations of what they learn. Each section is designed to offer them very helpful information.

Chapter 8: Strengthening

This chapter also covers a lot of territory and includes many scriptural references. Because of its length, you probably will need to "hit the high points" during your class discussion. For example, you might ask participants what key points they derived from each subheading, rather than read each Scripture. Ask, "What can *you* learn from the schoolhouse of suffering?" or, "What Scripture helped you to mine gold from the pits?"

Chapters 8 and 9 offer crucial principles for helping participants reinforce their faith and move ahead with their lives. Explain that while you cannot possibly cover every detail within the time constraints of the class, their workbooks will be valuable resources for years to come.

Chapter 9: Praying

Hopefully, at this point in your study, you will notice a general change among participants in how prayer is perceived. Some participants who were hesitant about sharing prayer concerns may be more open now. Others will begin to see the beneficial effects of prayer on their lives. All should acknowledge the need for and blessing of prayer. In addition to explaining the reasons for prayer, Chapter 9 offers a good lesson in how to pray. You thus will be helping to train praying women. Prayer is important to all people in all circumstances, but it is especially comforting and strengthening to widows.

Make time to conclude this lesson with a special time of prayer. If you have not been asking for prayer requests each week, make an exception and include them this time.

Chapter 10: Forgiving

Do not be fooled by the brevity of this chapter. Forgiveness is a touchy subject and must be handled with great sensitivity. People who thought they had forgiven someone are often shocked by their own feelings of bitterness and anger. Some may think they have "moved on," but still harbor resentment against God for taking their loved ones from them.

At this point in your study, your participants should feel enough freedom to share their thoughts and feelings. Allow ample time for dialogue, but always be ready to move the discussion forward. "The Rest of the Story" may bring up some difficult aspects of a relationship. Participants have a choice in how they will respond. Focus on forgiveness as an attitude that has to be developed and exercised.

Chapter 11: Appreciating

Like forgiveness, gratitude is a life-enhancing tool. This chapter should have resulted in a positive week for your participants, a week of reflecting on all that is good in their lives and all they have to be thankful for. Hopefully, your participants have grown enough through this study to be able to give thanks for some aspects of their lives. Not everyone will enjoy the same degree of gratitude, of course. It will take some women longer to achieve an appreciative mind-set. Continue to encourage them and point the way, showing patience and kindness to those who are not there yet.

Chapter 12: Choosing

Throughout this study, you have emphasized the importance of choice—choice of perspective, choice of attitude, choice of response. That is the crux of this chapter and the crux of their individual journeys. Will they choose to go forward? Do they understand that their choices every day affect where they will end up?

Because of the length of this chapter, you may decide to focus on key points under each subheading. Time will not permit you to read all the Scriptures, but do try to select key verses, or ask participants which Scriptures meant the most to them.

Chapter 13: Living On

This is the "bird ready to leave the nest" chapter. Are your participants ready to live in a healthier way? Are they focusing on the right things? Do they understand the importance of their decisions and their actions?

Encourage them to write you a note about how they are going to "Live On." What decisions have they made as a result of this study?

Please have them complete an evaluation of this study. Your input and theirs are critical to helping us improve this study for future participants. Your input and theirs are important to us. We will read your evaluations. We will address your concerns.

Please give them our love and tell them our prayers will follow them.

LEADER EVALUATION AND SUGGESTIONS

We need your feedback to make this study as effective as possible for all concerned. We see you as our eyes and ears to give us critical input for improvement in order to meet the needs of those involved. Please let us know your thoughts.

1. Did you gain anything from this study?

2. What would have aided you in your leadership of this study?

3. What did you think was the most beneficial part of this study?

4. Where did you see room for improvement and how would you implement this improvement?

5. What feedback did you get from your participants?

Any comments are welcomed and will be prayerfully addressed.

With our gratitude for all you did to help support and bless widows!

PARTICIPANT EVALUATION AND SUGGESTIONS

1. What did you gain from this study?

2. What would have helped you benefit more from this study?

3. What would you like to see added or eliminated from this study?

4. What did you see as the strength of this study?

Any comments or suggestions are appreciated. They will be prayerfully addressed.

Thank you so much for your involvement in this study.
Our prayer is that you will be served and blessed by this study and your group.

QUOTE INDEX

NOTES

SCRIPTURE INDEX

TOPIC INDEX

NOTES